TRUE SELF

Thriving Through Adversity

NICOLE NJIKE-BOBGA

WESTBOW
PRESS®
A DIVISION OF THOMAS NELSON
& ZONDERVAN

WestBow Press books may be ordered through booksellers or by contacting:

WestBow Press
A Division of Thomas Nelson & Zondervan
1663 Liberty Drive
Bloomington, IN 47403
www.westbowpress.com
844-714-3454

ISBN: 979-8-3850-3914-2 (sc)
ISBN: 979-8-3850-3916-6 (hc)
ISBN: 979-8-3850-3915-9 (e)

Library of Congress Control Number: 2024925030

Print information available on the last page.

WestBow Press rev. date: 11/26/2024

DEDICATION

This book is dedicated to my mother, Njike Justine, who prematurely passed away nine years ago. I also dedicate it to all the ladies who passed away without fulfilling their divine purposes. I pray that we ladies who are still alive may receive strength, courage, and wisdom to fulfill our own God-ordained destinies. May we also not be afraid of the unknown but courage to believe in the abilities that God has placed in each of us as overcomers.

CONTENTS

INTRODUCTION

It was a hot day in a small city called Limbe in Cameroon, a country on the Gulf of Guinea in West and Central Africa. Cameroon is a bilingual country that was colonized by Britain and France in the 1900s. It was in the year 2000 that I, then ten years old, had left my mother, Njike Justine, and moved to live with my grandmother, Mafor Monica, to attend secondary school. "Ms. Njike," as her students used to call her, was an elementary school teacher. As the first daughter of a teacher, I always had to be in the spotlight when it came to education. At the First School Leaving Certificate (FSLC) and Common Entrance (CE) examinations, the two exams of primary school that qualify a person for secondary school for those who are used to the British system of education, I did so well, I was ranked best student in mathematics in the Southwest region of Cameroon.

My grandma lived in a section of her first daughter's house (my step-aunt) separate from the main house. After six months of living here, I caught measles, a contagious viral disease spread through respiratory droplets of infected individuals. It presents with a rash that starts on the face and behind the ears, then spreads to the rest of the body. With this, I couldn't go to school. I was being treated with roadside medicines to treat malaria and some paracetamol (called Tylenol here in the United States) that my grandma bought. A week passed and I couldn't go to school because the measles kept getting worse and the rashes had spread all over my body. With this fever and rashes all over my body, I was itchy and hot. I remember how I was so hot at one point in time that I had to pour water on the cement floor and just lay on it just to cool off. I was home alone as my grandma had a small business where she sold bananas on the street down the road.

Three more days passed, and my classmates started wondering why I was not in school. Lying on the cool cement to cool off had become a coping habit for me. Lying on the floor, I heard some voices that I recognized. Those were my two classmates, Linda and Maureen, who had come to find out why I had not been to school and to tell me that exams were starting the next week. Seeing me lying on the floor, weak and pale, they offered to take me to the hospital. When we arrived at the hospital, the doctors offered to admit me for better treatment, but my step-aunt refused, saying there was no one to take care of me if I was admitted since they were all busy. The doctor gave me some medications, but I don't remember their names. These made me feel better. I was then sent home with some home medications. This was a Wednesday.

I took these medications and for the next couple of days, and I felt much better. I couldn't be more grateful for these two friends of mine. Without them, I don't know how the next couple of days would have been for me. Everyone left the house in the morning and returned just in the evening to find out how I was feeling. It had been two weeks since I had last been to school. The following Monday, I arrived at school, and it was test week. *Where do I begin?* I asked myself. I got lost trying to remember the last topic taught or catching up with the ones missed. Before I knew it, our chemistry teacher, Mrs. Enyong, walked into class and said, "Put away all your books, for we are about to begin our test." Panic struck me. I felt dizzy and anxious as I asked myself, *Should I walk up to her and tell her I cannot take the test because I was sick and out of school for the past two weeks?* Then, I looked at her stern face as she looked at every student making sure his or her book was put away. *She won't give me a listening ear;* I said to myself. I decided to sit and fill out my test paper with all the knowledge I had.

"I will be passing the test papers," she said, "and do not start writing until I tell you to do so." After ensuring that all the students had copies of the test, she then wrote the start and end time for the test on the blackboard. This test was to last for forty-five minutes. As I looked at my test paper, I felt dizzy. Then I remembered that I had drunk my morning medications without eating anything. I scribbled a few answers on the first two questions and—boom—there came the urge to puke. I rushed to the teacher and told her I wasn't feeling too well. She asked in a typical African teacher's voice, "Then what do you want me to do now?"

Hearing this response, the urge to puke came even more intensely. I tried to hold it back but, nope, it would not stay down. I rushed out while lifting a finger to Mrs. Enyong in an attempt to excuse myself. Seeing me holding my hand to my mouth in an attempt to catch my puke, she signaled for me to leave the class. After relieving myself, I sat on a block outside the class. I observed some ants moving together in a straight line as they carried their food. A few of them kept going back and forth but made sure they came back to line up with the others and continue on their journey. After about ten minutes of observing them, I compared myself to these few ants that went back and forth but still found their way back in line. I said to myself, *I think I am better off going back to class and lining up like my other classmates by taking the test like them. A test paper filled with something is better off than a blank one.* I went to the nearby water tap, washed my face, drank some water, and went back to class.

As I walked into the class, I felt more determined than ever before. I sat on my bench, took my pen, and wrote down all that I could remember from past lectures and notes. When the teacher announced that there were fifteen minutes left, I wrote as fast as I could until I was able to answer my last question. As she picked up the test papers, I felt a sigh of relief that at least I wasn't turning in a blank paper. It was an all-week test, so I managed to get the majority of the lessons missed in other subjects from my classmates. For these other tests, I was not too anxious because I had at least reviewed the material.

Two weeks later, Mrs. Enyong handed back the test papers with their scores. She handed them according to performance, starting from the highest to the lowest score. Guess what? My name was the first to be called. I was the top scorer on this test with a score of eighteen out of twenty points. Can you believe this? The entire class was surprised and so was I. Until this day, I don't know how that happened. One thing I know is that God did it for me. Then, I asked myself what if I had given up on this test? What if I had let my current illness determine my failure in this test? What if, what if, what if? In the second trimester, I did well in the subsequent tests and subjects and was the top of my class. Can you believe this? This marked the beginning of a great testimony in my academic journey.

I attempted to let my illness stop me from taking my tests. I assumed that my teacher would understand me and offer me the opportunity to take the test later. Similarly, there are many times when we assume that the world will understand us and treat us kindly based on our current or past situations. Nope! Sometimes, life will place people on your path who will make you question the humane nature of people just like that of my chemistry teacher. Many times, we feel stuck in situations and become blinded by the circumstances that surround us. Permit me to ask these questions. How many times have we let the circumstances in which we find ourselves determine our courses of action and either good or bad results? How many times have we just given up on ourselves, our children, our spouses, our families, and our friends because we faced obstacles that deterred us from our goals and future plans? How many times have we stayed frustrated and stuck in one spot because things didn't go as planned? How many times, how many times, how many times?

To a reader of this book, I pray that the inspiration I received from the ants, as well as the subsequent stories in this book, will help stir up your spirit and faith. I hope that you will be uplifted enough to step out of your current circumstances and step into the future that awaits you—the future that you have so desperately wanted for yourself and your loved ones. Selah!

Dear saints reading this book, please permit me to introduce myself. My name is Nicole Njike-Bobga and I was born in the late 1980s in Limbe, Cameroon. I am the second of seven siblings and the first girl, technically the second mother of the house. My mom, being a single parent, raised me alongside my six other siblings. When I completed elementary school, my grandma pleaded with my mom to allow me to come live with her so I could be of help to her as she was getting older. That was how I left my mom and went to live with my grandma, with whom I spent seven years of my life. After that, I went to university back in Buea, where I originally lived with my mom.

In this book, I am going to be sharing stories about my personal life experiences, my walk with Christ, the challenges I faced, and how God helped me overcome them. I hope that after someone reads this book, he or she will believe and trust that the power of God can really be made manifest in the lives of whomever believes in Him.

Before we dive into this book, I would like to share how the vision for writing this book came about. During my twenty-one-day fast in January 2023, the Lord placed it in my heart to write about my life, all that I have been through, and how I overcame these difficulties. The Lord specifically instructed me to write the book and have it published on the day of my tenth wedding anniversary. At the time He said this, I had just thirty dollars in my bank account. My first questions to Him were, "Lord, how do I pour out my private life in public? Who will believe me, especially knowing that I grew up on another continent? Explaining my childhood and past stories in a different environment, who will understand me or believe me?" I went further and asked, "Where will I have the money to produce the book since I have just thirty dollars in my bank account?" He did not answer me. Then, I knew that His silence meant I had doubted him and the power of His might.

Reluctantly, I proceeded to inquire about the process involved in writing and producing a book. I watched many YouTube videos to guide me in this process. I attended seminars on how to write and publish a book. I then stumbled on one renowned author who helps direct people on their book writing processes. I booked a meeting just to know what the process entails and how much it would cost. In this meeting, we spoke about the time, commitment, and cost involved. After this meeting, I went to God and asked Him, "God, You are telling me to write this book. First, if I have to write a book, this is going to be my first. I will have to work with a good producer who will provide me with adequate guidance since I will not want to write any kind of jargon about the Lord. Not only that, but I also do not have the thousands of dollars required to pay for the production of a good book. I do not even see myself having it by the day You want me to publish it."

The Lord answered me with these three words: "I will provide." I felt peace within me after hearing the most reassuring words from the most important being on earth and in Heaven. His voice felt like a gentle peace that calmed the storm of doubtful thoughts and questions flooding my mind as I poured out the many obstacles surrounding my current situation. These words from Him were to fulfill one aspect of His character and personality: Jehovah Jireh, the Lord my provider. As written in Philippians 4:19 (KJV), "But my God shall supply all your needs according to His riches in glory by Christ Jesus." I then read books to guide me on how to start drafting a manuscript. As I read the books, ideas of what to write and how to draft my manuscript began to flood my mind. I wrote down everything I remembered. I remember how the Holy Spirit placed it in my heart to include a particular story about my life. I asked Her, "Don't you think that is a little too personal?" I felt like I would be exposing the people involved in the story. Then, I started pondering how to write the story in an edifying way and not in a condemning way. Regardless, I still jotted down my ideas. Months passed as I struggled to write my manuscript while managing two jobs, a family of four kids, a husband, school, and preparing for my tenth wedding anniversary. It was very challenging, and I felt frustrated several times in the process. Then, I remembered God's promises of His provision. I said to myself that if God said He was going to provide for me to produce this book, He was going to equip me with the strength, knowledge, wisdom, and finances needed to write this book while accomplishing all the other stuff in my life.

Amidst the challenging situations, I barely had time to edit my manuscript or add more ideas. Since I was running out of time, I sought ways to make this possible. One of these ways was to use speech to text to write my ideas as I drove. I had a job where I drove three and a half hours to go to work four times in a month. I used this driving time to speak all the ideas for this book and send them to myself. When I arrived at my destination, I would copy and paste whatever I had written into my manuscript. Then I would look for time to edit my work. I used this method to write a lot of the material in this book. I used several other methods to enable me complete and publish this book at the time stipulated by God.

Unfortunately for me, with all my efforts, I could not meet the deadline. I felt so depressed because first, I had failed God and, second, as a go-getter, I felt disappointed in myself. I told God that maybe this was not meant to be or maybe someone else should complete this task. I kept going back and forth with the "what ifs" or "what if nots." One day, I was listening to a preacher, Terri Savelle Foy, who told the story behind her book-writing process and the obstacles she faced. She still published her book amidst these circumstances. I researched the challenges that authors faced, and I was overwhelmed by what I saw. These authors overcame them and ended up publishing their books. I said to myself, *I am not the only one facing these challenges. The only difference between them and me is that they have successfully published their books while I haven't. Therefore, I have to step up my game.*

I set a deadline of two months to publish this book. This deadline passed and I had not even turned in my manuscript. Here I was again discouraged. Then, an angel of God Almighty came to me in a dream and held my hand, saying, "Be encouraged. You can do it." As I woke up from that dream, I was extraordinarily encouraged and determined. I had to set aside time to complete this book. About two weeks later, I submitted my manuscript. The editing continued from there until here we are with the finished product.

Hey sister! Hey brother! You reading this book, I want to encourage you today not to give up on that dream that God has placed in your heart. One thing I have learned is that on judgment day, God will hold us more accountable for what we did not do than for what we did. Yes, you heard me right! In the end, what we failed to do can cost us a lot more than what we did. My prayer for us all is that we should never be discouraged from putting in all it takes to do what God has called us to do. God has an unlimited supply of help for us. All we need to do is to call unto Him to grant us access to this help supply. One thing I have learned is that there is a level of exposure when God has allowed you access, He would not want you to keep it to yourself. He will require you to share it with the world. He will provide you with all the resources needed to accomplish your goals, even if it means making you do them against your own will. This was the story of Jonah in the Bible, and this is my and your story. I pray that this book will serve the purpose for which God intended for me to write it. May this book be an eternal blessing to you and me as we journey through life in Christ Jesus. Amen.

CHAPTER 1

VENGEANCE

*Vengeance robs you of your innocence, exposing you
to Satan's accusation and to God's judgment.*

Kong Qiu, also known as Confucius, a Chinese philosopher, once said, "Before you embark on a journey of revenge, dig two graves: one for you and the other for the person you want to carry out the revenge on."

The society in which we live today can be so provocative. It can be challenging to maintain a non-strenuous relationship with others. In the process, defamation of another person's character, revenge seeking, and many other ungodly ways have become the order of the day. As someone filled with the Holy Spirit, it is important that you do not seek revenge against those who have offended you. When someone hurts you to the point where you have the urge to repay them in their very own coins to quench your thirst for being hurt, remember 1 Thessalonians 5:15 (NIV): "Make sure that nobody pays back wrong for wrong, but always strive to do what is good for each other and for everyone else." The Holy Spirit is reminding us today that vengeance is of the Lord. You accumulate grace for yourself for being innocent despite being hurt, and for not carrying out revenge despite having all the reasons to. This is not because what they did to you didn't hurt your feelings or affected your life. It is because you did not seek to repay the person back in his or her own coins. There's a special grace available for those who have been hurt and betrayed. You can only benefit from that grace if you yourself remain pure by not seeking vengeance and let God fight for you.

The word of God says in Exodus 14:14 (NIV), "The Lord will fight for you; you need only to be still." To be still means to maintain deep silence and calm, make no sound, or remain quiet. Did you get that? I sure did because that felt like a word for me particularly. Just like people move around with different kinds of grace, so too people move around with different kinds of demonic spirits. Most often, these spirits that people carry are responsible for causing the hurt and pain. Seeking vengeance on these people can result in hurting these people rather than the spirits responsible for their acts. Some carry spirits of marital confusion. When they step foot into your home, you will find yourself arguing with your spouse over trivial things. Many other things you may observe when some people show up in your life. Most often, these people don't even know that they carry these spirits.

Let me take a minute and pray for us. According to God's word in Obadiah 1:17 (KJV), "But upon mount Zion shall be deliverance, and there shall be holiness; and the house of Jacob shall possess their possessions." Therefore, I command any, and all evil spirits inhabiting our bodies, with or without our consent, to let us loose right now in the powerful name of Jesus. I bring these spirits to submission at the feet of Jesus Christ. I declare us free in Jesus's name. As we express our freedom in Christ, we possess all that was stolen from us in the powerful name of Jesus Christ. Amen.

In the same way, we have people who move around with various graces. These may include marital grace, grace for ease, or grace for fertility. Every time they are around you, you find that past difficult things can be easily accomplished, and you become fertile in many areas in your life.

That is why it is important that, every now and then, we do a personal deliverance, which starts with *repentance*. Usually, we invite these evil spirits into ourselves either through our ways of life, the words that come out of our mouths, our interactions, the places we visit, the company we keep, and even our very own thoughts. For example, before becoming a professional robber, a person starts by stealing one item. If not caught, that person steals another item and then another. Then, the devil sees that this person is open to stealing and he can inhabit the person's body. The person can then serve the devil through stealing. In this situation, this person's way of life (stealing) is what attracted the devil to him or her because, ideally, no one is a born thief.

When you feel like carrying out vengeance on someone who has hurt you, choose to defer what you prefer and let God take control. Yes! It is our default tendency to want to hurt people who have hurt us. By ourselves, we cannot hold back from seeking vengeance. That is why we have scriptures and the Holy Spirit to help us in such weaknesses. Scripture tells us in Proverbs 20:22 (GNBDC), "Don't take it on yourself to repay a wrong. Trust the LORD and he will make it right." God's delayed vengeance is by far better than our quick or hurried vengeance. Which do you prefer? Do you want to hurry and carry out a vengeance that sometimes ends in failure, causing you to be ridiculed or humiliated? Or would you rather wait on God to do it for you? It is important to note that if God wants to carry out vengeance, He doesn't need our help. He will do it in a way that best pleases Him. For instance, He can decide to punish the perpetrator severely or He can cause that person to learn from his or her mistakes. He can give the person the opportunity to correct himself or herself in future relationships. Better still, God can do whatever He chooses with that person. God created us to love us unconditionally and to protect His name. At the end of the day, whatever He chooses to do will save us or the other person from harm and give glory to His name.

I have noticed that when someone hurts me and I decide to move on without carrying out revenge, some might think I am foolish and did not see what the other person did. Others think I am holding grudges against the person, or I am planning something evil against him or her. Rather, I know that because the person committed such acts against me, I can no longer trust that person fully or hold him or her close at heart like I did before. I learn to set boundaries between us based on what the person just did to me. Setting boundaries does not mean holding grudges; rather, it means you no longer want to create that proximity that can make such betrayal repeat itself. You learn from that experience and make the necessary adjustments to protect your mental health. Have you ever decided not to carry out vengeance against someone who has hurt you and show the person love instead? Was that person afraid to come near you because he or she thought you were just faking the forgiveness and planning something evil? The person has become afraid of you. I have had situations where people who have offended me become frightened when they see me, especially if they were not expecting to see me. Such people are already going through psychological trauma on their own and that is more traumatizing than vengeance against them.

Personally speaking, whenever someone hurts me, I want to take revenge so badly, with my heart beating so fast as I plan how to execute my vengeance. As I reflect on my plans, guilt will set in, and I ask myself what I am doing. Then, I cry out to God, saying, "God, I need deliverance more than I need vengeance. Help me overcome this in Jesus's name Amen." Then I start to beg for forgiveness from God for even having this thought in the first place. The Bible says, "As a man thinketh in his heart so is he" (Proverbs 23:7 KJV). The only thing that separates the thought from the vengeance is the *act*. I implore us all to try out this strategy whenever the deluge of vengeance comes knocking on our doors. Since this has worked for me, I firmly believe it will work for you too in Jesus's name. Amen.

In the past, I would rain insults on the perpetrators, and my best way of doing this was through text messages. However, as I become more mature in kingdom things, I have learned to give a grace period for everyone who offends me. Have you ever heard the saying that the test for good manners is to be patient with bad ones? Yes, I am patient with the bad ones until I see that the perpetrator is doing things intentionally. By grace period, I mean I will let the person's first hurtful act slide by with the hope that he or she can reflect on it later and adjust his or her ways toward me and possibly others. Sometimes, this works for some people. At other times, these offenders keep hurting me, thinking my silence means I am weak or guilty. In these cases, rather than engaging in a fight with them, I request to meet with them or call them if meeting is not possible. When you request to meet with such people, it is important to note that confronting evil is not tidy, so don't expect the talk to be a smooth one. In the meeting or over the phone, I voice my complaints about how their actions hurt my feelings. In some cases, they will repent and ask for forgiveness, tell me the reason for their actions, or explain that I prompted them to behave that way. In other cases, some people will refuse to admit their faults and rain down more insults on me. In these cases, I take my stand and know how I will interact with them subsequently or draw necessary boundaries as needed. In these cases, I need not carry out any revenge because, if I do, I am no different from them.

Whenever you think of doing something wrong against someone who has offended you, ask yourself these questions: What am I building? Whose kingdom am I building? Not seeking vengeance does not mean you are weak. Instead, it means you have mastered yourself and the power of Christ in you so well that you don't let evil overpower you because vengeance is evil. Not seeking revenge means you have power, and your standards are higher than vengeance. Whatever begins in anger, ends in shame. Vengeance feels right in the beginning, but in the end, it will yield more shame and pain.

There are moments when it is necessary to confront someone who has hurt you and there are moments when all you need is to be still. Confrontation does not mean you engage in a dirty argument with the person. Instead, you can plan a meeting with that person so you two can have a conversation. Then, you voice how you have been hurt by that person's actions. In this scenario, there are only two ways the person will react. He or she will apologize and repent or add salt to injury by denying his or her actions or giving you senseless justifications. In either way, this will determine your next course of action and therefore your relationship with the person. Even the Bible tells us to "Give at least two warnings to those who cause divisions, and then have nothing more to do with them. You know that such people are corrupt, and their sins prove that they are wrong" (Titus 3:1011 GNBDC). In the end, you will be more blessed because you don't treat people the way they treated you.

When I say set up a meeting with the person, I don't mean setting this every time the person offends you. Some things are better off being cleared off on the spot. However, you have to weigh things and determine your ideal course of action. Setting up a meeting is ideal for something that someone repeatedly does, and you want to make sure you stop it once and for all. Either way, you still want to drive your point while maintaining your integrity as a child of God.

Let's relive a story in the Bible in Genesis chapter 34. Dinah was the daughter of Leah and Jacob. When Jacob left his father-in-law to go to the land of his father, they stopped to rest in a city called Shalem in the land of Canaan. Dinah went to visit the daughters of this city. Shechem, the son of

Hamor, the prince of the land, saw her and defiled her. When her brothers heard about this, they were furious. Such a thing was an abomination in Israel. Then Hamor, the father of Shechem pleaded with them and Jacob to give Dinah in marriage to Shechem and to also marry the other women in the tribe to their boys. The brothers deceitfully told Hamor that they would agree to this on the condition that all the men in the land become circumcised as they themselves were circumcised. Hamor and his son Shechem were pleased with this response. They believed they had struck a great deal and convinced all their men to be circumcised. Three days after their circumcision, when the men were sore, Jacob's two sons, Simeon and Levi, slaughtered all the males in retaliation for the defilement of their sister. They knew the men were sore and had limited capacity to fight. They killed Hamor and Shechem and took their cattle and wealth. When Jacob heard this, he was devastated at what they had done. The boys replied, "Should he treat our sister like a prostitute?" These boys took matters into their hands, carried out vengeance, and eliminated an entire city because of the wrong that one man did to their sister.

However, this single act cost them and their children a lot in later years when their father, Jacob, was blessing them on his dying bed. In Genesis chapter 49, Jacob reminded Simeon and Levi about their act against the people of Shechem and told them that his soul would not be joined to their counsel because of their anger. Their generation would be divided and scattered in Israel. Their birthright status and preeminence passed over them and went to the fourth son of Jacob, Judah. What they had done threatened the family unit and Jacob remembered this on his deathbed. Though killing the men of Shechem gave relief to Simeon and Levi at that moment, I can imagine them when it cost them blessings from their father. These same brothers saw the love that their brother, Joseph, was getting from their father. They became jealous of him and sought to kill him but ended up selling him into slavery. Nemesis caught up with them as Joseph fed and catered to them during the years of famine. Joseph never sought to exact vengeance on his brothers for what they did to him. Again, Jacob remembered this and gave distinct blessings to Joseph and his two sons Ephraim and Manasseh. Imagine that Joseph, after becoming second in command in Egypt, went back to his father's land to mock his brothers. Most of us, including me, could have done that if we were in Joseph's place.

However, Joseph forgot about them and accepted his fate until destiny brought his brothers to him. Joseph, though hurt, never went back to them.

The thirst for vengeance increases the more you practice it. This means that the more you carry out revenge, the more you will want to carry it out to maintain your vengeance status quo. However, it is important to note that carrying out vengeance is a choice. With every choice comes blessings or consequences. Simeon and Levi were cursed for their choice of vengeance while Joseph was blessed for his choice of forgiveness (not carrying out vengeance). The choice is ours. Forgiveness does not mean going to look for those who offended you to tell them you have forgiven them. Moving forward with your own life, staying in your lane, going about your business, and not even thinking about them is a good way of living. After Jacob (their father) died, Joseph's brothers were afraid that he was going to carry out revenge against them. Joseph replied that what they meant for evil, God meant it for good.

Pamela Short, a mental health first aid instructor, stated, "The best revenge is none. Heal, move on and don't become like those who hurt you."[1] I completely agree with this saying because life always has its ways of repaying people who have wronged you, no matter how long it takes. God has the capacity to use an evil act done toward you to your advantage, just like he did for Joseph. When next you and I think of carrying out vengeance, let's remember that we might be ruining our chances of receiving a blessing from God. When someone who has offended us genuinely seeks forgiveness, it is a holy choice to forgive him or her.

Let me elaborate on two scenarios I encountered in the past to enable you to better appreciate what I mean. Years ago, I worked as a nurse in a clinic in Cameroon. One weekend, my friends and I were partying and were on our way home when we were attacked by thieves in my neighborhood. This happened in front of the homes of police officers. Knowing this, I screamed for help by calling one of the officers' names. I hoped he would rescue us. The thieves became so mad and came back after me. God alone knows how I was able to run in the dark on almost four-inch-high heels and escaped from these thieves. In return, these thieves furiously went back and assaulted my other friends to the point of defiling

[1] "Pamela Short Quotes," Goodreads, accessed November 5, 2024, https://www.goodreads.com/author/quotes/14997571.Pamela_Short.

one of them. After this incident, I felt so guilty for this act and spent a considerable amount of time comforting my friends, especially the one who was defiled. I remember spending numerous nights at her place, doing her laundry and helping her with her house chores. All seemed to be all right and we both returned to work as usual. Unfortunately for me, all was not over in my friend's heart as she became bitter toward me.

I was taking over leadership as the clinic administrator from her as she had been hired by the government and had to quit. Before leaving, this friend used her harbored bitterness to influence the rest of the staff not to show me respect. She encouraged people to believe I didn't deserve the position and that our boss just put me in that position because I was the most qualified staff for the moment. When I took over leadership, the atmosphere changed. Whatever policy was in place was disregarded by some of the staff, especially those who were close friends with her. One particular staff member had become very close to my said friend before her departure. This staff member took it upon herself to humiliate and disrespect me in front of everyone, including patients. I complained to the boss, who cautioned her to no avail. The boss said we should lay her off, but I told my boss to hold on and give her another chance. This happened after I discovered that she had been receiving evil counsel from my predecessor. I prayed about this, and the Lord directed me to read His word in Matthew 18:15–17 (GNBDC).

> "If your brother sins against you, go to him and show him his faults. But do it privately, just between yourselves. If he listens to you, you have won your brother back. But if he will not listen to you, take one or two other persons with you, so that every accusation may be upheld by the testimony of two or more witnesses. And if he does not listen to them, tell the whole thing to the church. Finally, if he will not listen, treat him as though he were a pagan or a tax collector."

With this, I told my boss one morning about a plan I had for that staff member. I did exactly as scripture commanded. I called her and talked things out with her, emphasizing how I wanted us to work as a team to make this clinic grow. That she should forgive me if I had done anything to offend her. After listening to me, she walked out of the room and slammed the door on me. Weeks later, her negative attitude became even worse. In one incident, after coming to work, she abandoned her duties and went shopping at a nearby market. My boss and I issued her a quarrel letter. She replied to this letter, not addressing the issues mentioned in the letter. Instead, she outlined the weaknesses she said I also had and indicated that I had no reason to judge her. With all the reasons to lay her off, the Lord reminded me about His word. I held my peace and called another meeting with three other staff who knew about the situation. During the meeting, I explained all the disrespect that this particular staff had been showing toward me and how I had no grievances against her. I read her reply to the quarrel letter to the others. The staff present attested that they, too, had noticed her poor behavior toward me and counseled her on how inappropriate this was. In the meeting, she said she bore no grudges against me. They asked her why she behaved like this if she had no grudges. She said she felt that I hated her. They explained to her how I had every reason to hate her, rather, I showed her love; she was the one showing the hate. In front of the other staff, I personally told her that I did not hate her, and I wanted us to work in harmony. After this meeting, she became calm and was respectful toward me.

About a month later, she became a worse version of her older self and disrespected me in front of the patients. I went to church and told God everything about how I had obeyed His command and implemented His word. Because all my efforts were ineffective, He should be the judge between me and this individual. A few weeks later, this staff member had a myomectomy at our clinic. A couple of days later, she was discharged. A few days later, she returned to the clinic with profuse vaginal bleeding. She was readmitted to the clinic. A couple of days later, the bleeding subsided, and she was discharged again. She later on resumed work. Barely two days after resuming work, she had another episode of bleeding that was worse than before. My boss asked for my help because he was not able to locate the bleeding site in the uterus. He had tried everything within his power to stop the bleeding, all of which had failed. He was afraid she might pass out. It was a chaotic moment as all the other staff members became afraid at the way she was losing blood. I went into the room where she lay helpless on the examination table. I suggested a shot that I had seen given to patients to stop bleeding when I worked in a bigger hospital. When they brought the shot, I made a prayer and administered the shot. At once, she stopped bleeding. With the help of another staff, we cleaned her up, padded her, and helped her to a room to rest.

After this incident, I remember one of the staff asking me, "So Nicole, you still went ahead and touched this girl's blood after all that she has done to you?'

I replied, "Darkness can never conquer light." A day later, she was discharged. When she returned to work, all we could see was guilt on her face and she could barely look me in the eyes. This was the turning point for this staff member. She never showed these inappropriate behaviors toward me again. Two weeks later, the Lord blessed me, and I was offered a job in another city at four times my current salary. My boyfriend proposed to me, and we wedded five months later. I conceived on my wedding night and had my son a day before my birthday (the best birthday gift ever)! On one of my visits to this former clinic, my former boss told me that within one year, God had blessed me with what other women take years to achieve. One thing I know is this was the hand of God working in my life and especially because I obeyed God's word.

From this story, we can see that God carried out vengeance on my behalf. I had decided to carry out vengeance initially and was planning to either beat her up or fire her as my boss had suggested. Beating her up would have meant she could have accused me later of being the cause of her bleeding. This could have been a stain on my personality or maybe a police case. On the other hand, firing her would have caused her to point an accusing finger at me for causing her to lose her job. Letting God do the fighting for me was so edifying because it caused this individual to repent. Most importantly, it taught me patience.

With this story, I want us to see how one person's lack of forgiveness and zeal for vengeance caused another person to become toxic and cause the other person to suffer.

In my walk with God and my relationships with people, I have noticed that some people are so weak when it comes to being convinced to hate another person, even if this person has not done anything wrong to them. Whenever I see people believing a story by listening to just one side of it, I just know these people lack the spirit of discernment. In chapter 5, we are going to talk more about the spirit of discernment.

Another incident involved a lady who watched my kids while I went to work. She also braided my hair. Later on, I had someone live with me to help me with my kids, and I didn't need to go leave my kids with the other lady. Moreover, I had just had a haircut and needed no braids. After a while, my hair grew, and I went to have my hair braided by this lady. As she braided my hair, she started teasing me about how I didn't let her watch my kids again or do my hair. She knew I would come back to her because she was my airport, meaning I could not do without her. She even mentioned the people I had now made friends with instead of her. She said many other prideful things. I stayed calm listening to her as she braided my hair. After that, I paid her and left. You may be wondering why I did not respond to her right away. Let me give you an answer.

I have learned that if I had answered her immediately, it would have resulted in physical fights with adequate fist exchanges, even to the point of calling the police. Knowing myself, I stayed calm and went home knowing that I would cool off. After I had cooled off, I would be able to talk to her in a more logical and edifying manner that would not involve any chaos. I would assume that in her heart, she knew she had dealt with me.

Weeks later after cooling off, I called her and requested to meet with her. She accepted and we met. I then regurgitated everything she had said and how angry that made me feel. I also told her if I had reacted then, it would have been total chaos. I then told her she needed to take some classes on how to talk to people, especially customers, knowing that I would pay her every time she watched my kids or braided my hair. As I was recounting all these things to her, she burst into tears and started weeping profoundly. She told me she just realized how foolish she had been and how sorry she was. She started telling me about her life's challenges and how she used the money I paid her to solve some of her problems. Because I was not coming to her anymore, all she felt toward me was resentment. Seeing me associating with people other than her made her feel more resentful. The following day, I woke up to a long message from her, which she sent at four in the morning. She said how grateful she was to me for coming to tell her personally and not spreading rumors about what she had done to other friends. After this, she became the humblest person, especially toward me.

She would greet me with respect, love, and affection whenever she saw me. Now imagine that I had reacted initially when she confronted me. I would have been narrating a different story now or not even mentioning it here at all.

From my personal experience, I have seen that I feel so good and do better when I have a one-on-one or tete-a-tete discussion with my offender instead of engaging in fights. In these fights, each partner can do hurtful things or tell lies just to win. Most often, things don't end well.

It is also important to note that sometimes some people will tell you they are sorry just because they are afraid. They fear that what they did to you will spread and they will have bad names. They are trying to cover it up, yet deep within themselves, they intend to repeat what they did far from human view. Those who tend to add salt to injury came into your life on a mission to destroy you.

Let me share another incident that happened between my husband and me and one of his friends. This friend basically lived in our home. Even though he had his own apartment, he would spend most of his days in our home. On days when he was busy, he would stop by our home after he was finished. On days he was not busy, he would spend almost the whole day at our home and return to his home only when he wanted to sleep. He had become a part of my family. He would tell us how he longed for a wife and to live as a wonderful couple just like me and my husband. I remember how my husband accompanied him to the store when he went to buy an engagement ring for the girl he was dating. Everything was going on smoothly until one day, he told us a female cousin and her daughter needed a place to stay. He asked if we could let them stay with us while she was waiting to get the keys to the apartment she was about to rent. This cousin and her daughter lived with us until she got the keys to her own apartment.

We later learned this cousin and her daughter had been chased from the home she was living in because she had attempted to seduce and date the husband of the home. The wife was furious and sent her and her daughter packing. When she came to us, we did not know the purpose for her departure from her previous home and welcomed her into our family. After she had lived with us for a couple of days, I felt in my spirit that something didn't feel right about her. I decided to hold my peace and just observe her. As time went by, I noticed that she preferred to associate with my husband rather than me. Even after she had moved into her own home, she stopped by to talk to my husband in the early hours of the morning before going to work. Everything felt right until things didn't feel right anymore. I asked her one time why she called my husband for favors rather than me. She replied that it was because she could never get through when she called me. I replied that my husband had the same phone and the same connection, and we were in the same location most often when she called. I combined my instincts with her behavior and decided to do a little more research about her.

I spoke with someone from where she used to live, and I was told about all the mishaps she had there and how she was chased by the wife of that home. I also prayed to God for guidance, knowing I didn't want to judge people based on their past mistakes. God vividly told me that this girl came to my house on a mission to destroy my home. With this information, I called her cousin who had brought her to my home and told him I never wanted to see her and daughter again anywhere near my home or my husband. Her cousin, on the other hand, took her side. Both of them started throwing provocative slang in the community WhatsApp group to which we all belonged. My husband and I decided to hold our peace as we watched the show. I said to myself she could throw those slang words here and only people who didn't know her would believe her. Moreover, she would only do this outside of my home and not in my home.

My husband later told me how his friend called him one day and told him he had brought two harlots to his place. My husband could come over if he wanted to come cool off with one of them since I was pregnant. He also told my husband how desperately he wanted his cousin to be documented since she was an undocumented immigrant. This outraged me as I imagined how I had been feeding someone who was on a mission to destroy my marriage. As time went by, these two cousins went to all the people we knew and spread lies about us. Knowing what the heart of a person is, most people believed their story. Again, this didn't move me knowing that I had taken my stand on what was right and knew who was protecting me. Her cousin, my husband's friend, even travelled to another city where we had previously lived, found some of my husband's old friends, and condemned us to them. One of these people then called my husband and revealed everything. My husband called his friend several times to talk to him, but he kept replying with a text that he was going to call back. Weeks would pass without him calling. I told my husband I was going to call him. I called but he would not pick up my calls.

I then decided to text him about everything he had said about us. He replied to me in a very provocative manner and showed no remorse. That made me even more furious. In return, I started raining insults on him until it turned into an insult party. He was very surprised at the things I told him because he never knew I was aware of the things he and his sister had done. He had no choice but to block my phone number. I messaged him on every social media platform and all he did was block me on them as well. He was running away because he knew what he had done and especially because we had discovered him. The hunter had become the hunted. Then, the Lord told me to stop insulting him because a child of God should not behave this way. I also remember the Holy Spirit in her gentle voice reminding me to not write to him again or look for him as this was not worthy of me as a child of God. Then, I stopped.

His cousin ended up relocating to another state with her daughter. She sent me a message apologizing for all that she had done to me, saying she treated me that way because I had accused her of wanting to befriend my husband. I did not respond to her. About three months later, she sent another text apologizing for everything. Again, I did not respond. Only God alone knows what He had done to her, but I leave that to her and her maker. To this day, her cousin has never shown any remorse.

Before all these events happened, I had a revelation about this my husband's friend. I dreamed how he died in a ghastly motor accident following what he did to me. His fiancé came crying to my door with so much sadness. After this dream, I called his fiancé and told her about it. I asked her to pray for him, knowing that we women can intercede for our spouses or spouses to be, and God will indeed answer us. I also cautioned the friend about this dream and prayed for him. In another dream, the Lord asked me to send that guy away from my home. Mind you, this was before any of these things had happened. I asked the Lord, "How do I chase away my husband's friend, especially knowing that he had not done anything to me at that time?" However, God had seen his heart and his plans toward my family. He ended up relocating and he has never shown any remorse.

In a debriefing, the Lord reviewed with me what I should have done. He said I shouldn't have told them about the dream because if He fulfills this dream now, accusatory fingers will be pointing toward me, holding me responsible for his misfortune. The Lord specifically told me if He tells me He is going to do something to someone who offended me, I should never tell that person. Here I was, a female version of Joseph who dreamt about the eleven stars (his brothers) bowing to him. His brothers became jealous of him. To me, I was hoping that telling him would make him adjust his ways and realize when he is about to do something foolish. God sent Jonah to warn the people of Nineveh; they listened to Jonah, repented, and were saved. I was hoping the same would happen to him. God made me understand that He alone chooses whom He will have mercy on and whom He will not. Though we may intercede and do our very best, only He has the final say. I learned that there are instances when you need to sit quietly, instances when you need to maturely confront someone, and instances in which you don't react further after confronting someone.

I don't know about you, but from my experiences, I have noticed that it takes more energy to carry out revenge than to seek a mature talk with your offender. Vengeance drains you of your positive energy and makes you utter words that you will live to regret. Personally, whenever I seek revenge, I can't even focus during my personal prayer sessions. Guilt kicks in and it takes me a long time to return to the same level of holiness or spirituality that I had before. Vengeance strips you of your innocence, exposing you to Satan's accusation and to God's judgment. Proverbs 28:10 (ESV) says that "the blameless will have a good inheritance." Even as we feel deeply hurt when someone offends us, let's make sure that our acts of retaliation or decisions keep us in a state of innocence. Honestly, if you are in your right senses, you will know when you have done evil or good. Sometimes, some of the things that people do to us are traps from the enemy so he can use our retaliation against us or against our children in the future. Let's be wise as we journey through life in Christ.

In my experience being married for the past ten years, I don't believe in one couple pausing their future just so another couple's future can be secured. This poses a high risk of danger to both couples and even to kids, in case anything negative should happen to a partner or that relationship. The future is at stake. By something negative, I mean not only divorce but diseases, kidnapping, sudden death, or any other adverse thing you can think of. Personally, I would recommend that couples weigh the importance of what they do and try to maintain a balance. What is more important for them as a couple at that time should be prioritized. What is trivial should be completed at a slower pace but *not completely neglected*. As a couple, you have to be proactive.

For example, after joining my husband in the United States, we wanted more babies. On the other hand, my husband had to go to school. He applied and was admitted to a pharmacy school. I was working and having babies as well. I knew I also wanted to pursue further education after my husband had finished his program and had a stable job. I started taking the prerequisite courses needed for the program I wanted to pursue. I took a couple of classes at a time, making sure to complete them at a pace that would be favorable to my family. I was working full-time and was making babies at the same time. Instead of two years to complete these courses, it took me three years because I had to accommodate our current situation. My husband graduated with his PharmD. About two years later, I graduated with an associate degree in biology and life sciences. He was starting to work and become grounded in his new career. At the same time, I was taking the next step toward achieving my dream career. I know a reader will say this is unimaginable. Yes, it is unimaginable but doable. Whether you get busy for yourself or for someone else, you are still going to be busy anyway. So why not get busy for the right thing, for what will benefit you, or for what you really like? Marriage or children could slow your pace of achieving your dreams but should never stop you from achieving them.

This is just my story. If you think you can't handle this type like me, find something else to do that will help you get where you want to be or be what you want to become. That way you will not have the fear of saying it's too late to start. With those associate degrees in my pockets, I know there's no backing down. I am only a few more steps away from achieving my dreams. This will make it easier for me to better prepare for my future adventure instead of starting from the beginning. The thought that you have to start from the beginning is discouraging. Do not think that this journey will be easy. I bet you it will be the scariest one ever, but the joy that comes from this accomplishment will be immeasurable. I also recommend seeking God's guidance at that time and the God who is all wise will instruct you on what to do. Trust Him and trust in the potential He has given you to accomplish all that you were placed on earth to do. Be that person who, when squeezed on one side, does not shrink but pops out on the other, unexpected side. Be like a balloon inflated with water with its tip tied. A gentle squeeze to the balloon makes the water move on the other side. More pressure forces it to burst and release itself to express its full content.

CHAPTER 2

THE "RETREVRES" ANOINTING

*Through repentance, God can use us or our generation
to accomplish great things that even those who didn't
commit such a sin will never be used to accomplish*

Through repentance, God can use us or our generation to accomplish great things that even those who didn't commit such a sin will never be used to accomplish.

Let's relive the story of King David and his military servant Uriah, according to 2 Samuel 11. David fell into the temptation of being intimate with Uriah's wife, Bathsheba, and she became pregnant. When she sent David a message about her pregnancy, David plotted Uriah's killing. After Uriah died, David took Bathsheba as his wife. The Bible tells us that what David did displeased the Lord. God sent the prophet Nathan to tell David a parable similar to what David had done to Uriah. David was so self-deceived that he was quick to pass judgment on the offender of Nathan's parable. David passed judgment on himself through his response to Nathan. Nathan exposed David by telling him that what he did to Uriah was the same thing the offender of the parable had done. Read 2 Samuel 12 for more on this story. God promised to punish David for this sin through four consequences. First, the sword would not depart from David's house, meaning there would be division and death in his family.

Second, David's wives would be taken away from him in a humiliating way. Third, God would raise up evil from within David's own household. Fourth, his child with Bathsheba would die. When David heard all these, he said to Nathan, "I have sinned against the Lord."

Nathan said to David, "The Lord also has put away your sin; you shall not die" (2 Samuel 12:13 ESV).

After Nathan left, David showed genuine repentance by fasting, praying, and begging God for forgiveness. The Bible tells us how David did not eat nor drink and lay on the floor until the baby passed away. David showed genuine repentance to God for his sins by being remorseful. Genuine repentance serves as evidence of a changed heart. When the baby died, David arose, took a shower, and then worshiped God. Wow! This is an act of believing that God has forgiven him and that he needed to take off his sinful old clothes and put on new clothes signifying redemption. He then went home and ate some food. When his servants asked him why he ate only after the child had died, David responded, "While the child was still alive, I fasted and wept, for I said, 'Who knows whether the Lord will be gracious to me, that the child may live?" (2 Samuel 12:22 ESV). After the baby died, David went to console Bathsheba, and he went into her. That was when she conceived Solomon, who later on became David's successor, the wisest king of all time. Let's take a second and give credit to Bathsheba as one very fertile woman. Maybe it was David who was a sharpshooter. How can a man go into a woman just once on two separate occasions and leave her pregnant? Wow! From David's story, I pray that we continually learn that when we sin, we should run to God and not from God. We are the ones who can't be trusted, not Him.

During one of my morning devotions while I was studying the Word of God, I was reading the book of Hosea chapter 6 verse 2. It talked about how the people decided to return to God after sinning against Him and God forgave their sins and accepted them back. This verse reminds us never to go away from God when He blesses us and even when we sin against Him. It also tells us that God wants us to be whole when we dwell in His presence. No infirmities should stop us from dwelling in His righteous presence. When God forgives our sins, He revives and restores us. *Revive* means to bring back to life or consciousness while *restore* means to bring you back to your rightful place. Many of us, though alive, are dead in many ways. Until God gives life back to you, He cannot restore you because you will not have the right mindset to manage all He will restore to you. We need to stay in His presence for His glory to continue to be made manifest in our lives. It is right to ask God to bless us all round when we are fully His, live in His presence, and walk according to His ways. I call this verse the "RevRes," anointing, a combination of the first three letters of the words *revival* and *restoration*. According to this verse, *revival* took place on the second day and *restoration* on the third day. What happened on the first day? Why does the Bible not mention what happened on the first day? If we read the first verse of Hosea chapter 6, we will see that the first day is the day the people made the decision to return to God. Everything starts with our hunger for repentance and change and decision to return to God. Just like David, may we never be afraid of coming to God whenever we sin. Perhaps the Lord will be gracious to us and refrain from punishing us.

When we show genuine repentance, God in his infinite mercy will certainly forgive us and spare our lives. It is important to note that when we sin, God can forgive our sins, but the consequences of our sins will remain with us. In David's case, even though God forgave him and spared him from dying, He still placed the four-fold consequences of his sins on him. It started with the baby's death and the remaining three consequences came to pass later in David's rule. Even after these consequences, God still had mercy on David and blessed him and Bathsheba with another son, Solomon, who later became David's heir. The Bible tells us how God loved Solomon so much that He sent a message through the prophet Nathan to name this boy Jedidiah, which means "beloved of the Lord." What a God! This is one of the times where we will say God's ways are not human ways. How could you kill the first-born child of Bathsheba and David to avenge the death of Uriah and then love another child from the same couple? What a God indeed!

Whenever I read these passages, I ask myself some questions. Could it be because the first child was born out of lust and murder? Could it be because God used this first child to avenge the death of Uriah? Could it be because David had repented and showed great remorse? Could it be something else? However, I firmly believe that after David showed genuine repentance, God in His infinite mercy decided to show mercy to David and Bathsheba by restoring them with a son. This son would be one God approved. That felt like a word for me. Whenever we try to have things our way, God can take them off or out and then replace them with His own version. God didn't give Bathsheba another girl or cause her to be barren. Rather, He blessed them with another version of a son that they had just buried—His own version.

The Bible does not mention Bathsheba's side of the story after she lost her baby. The Bible only mentions how David went to console her. However, I presume she was asking for forgiveness from both her dead husband Uriah and from God. Whatever the case, God answered their prayers and blessed them with another son. This means that after we have genuinely repented, God will certainly forgive our sins and execute the RevRes anointing by restoring us to our rightful places or giving us His own version of what He knows is best for us. There's nothing as sweet as God giving us a version of what He deems fit for us. What a joy! Let's give the RevRes anointing a new name: the RetRevRes anointing for return, revival, and restoration. I know you might be saying to yourself that what you have done is too grievous and not deserving of forgiveness. However, remember that the Bible says in Romans 10:10 (GNBDC), "It is by confession that we are saved."

If David had given excuses for his sins rather than beg for forgiveness from God, God would have certainly killed him. This is one of those scenarios that explains why God called David "a man after my heart." David killed almighty Goliath, lay on the floor in sack clothes for seven days, and starved himself in repentance before God. He didn't care if his servants saw him as absurd or mad. This is genuine repentance indeed. A similar thing happened with the prodigal son. After he realized that he had acted foolishly, he returned to his father and begged for forgiveness. His father killed the fatted calf to celebrate his repentance and comeback.

Just like David and the prodigal son, we too have the finest and fattest blessings that God has reserved for us if we return to him after sinning. Whenever we sin, let us never be shy or afraid to return to God and He will certainly restore to us our joyful inheritance. In the same way, whenever we discover that we have sought out vengeance or done anything that offends God, let us remember that we can always apply the RetRevRes anointing and strive not to return to our old ways. This is a continual process because we are constantly falling into sin. In our continual efforts to return to

God, God will give us new names such as "Beloved of the Lord." How sweet it is to move from "rejected" to "favorite!" Did you notice how the child who died had no name mentioned while the child that God loved, the child after repentance, God himself named? I call Solomon "the child of repentance" or "fruit of forgiveness." In subsequent scriptures, we see the kind of person Solomon turned out to be and God chose him to build His temple. Through repentance, God can use us or our generation to accomplish great things that even those who didn't commit such sin as ours will never be used to accomplish. I am a product of such! We all are!

CHAPTER 3

ARE YOU STRUGGLING TO MAINTAIN YOUR PRAYER LIFE?

Prayer is the difference between the best you
can do, and the best God can do.[2]
—Mark Batterson

Prayer is simply having an honest conversation with God. Prayer is not for
prayer warriors but for anyone who wants to be changed, edified, lifted, set
free, or made great in life. No one is born with the gift of prayer. No one is
born a prayer warrior. Prayer is learned. The more you pray, the more you
will know how to pray. During prayer, you do one or all of the following:
repent, converse, cry, and confront God. A Christian without prayer is
like a soldier without bullet-proof armor. He or she is like a dead person
standing. Stamina and consistency in prayer is built through repetition,
through the power of the Holy Spirit, and through constant study of and
meditation on the *Word of God*. Prayer is a keystone habit that propels
you to establish other holy habits. In my journey as an intercessor, I must
confess that prayer is one of the most inconvenient things I have had to do.

---

[2] Mark Batterson, *Draw the Circle: The 40 Day Prayer Challenge* (Grand Rapids, MI:
Zondervan, 2012), Chapter 23.

Imagine being well-tucked in bed, sleeping, and your alarm goes off at, let's say, 5:30 a.m., saying it's time to pray. This is especially true for those who set a prayer time. At this time, you were probably having the most deeply comfortable moment or dreams in your sleep. This may seem difficult, but it can become a habit where you just find yourself praying even as you sluggishly get out of bed. One thing that encourages me to pray is the scripture in which "Jesus told his disciples a parable to teach them that they should always pray and never become discouraged" (Luke 18:1 GNBDC). This means that without prayer, one can become easily discouraged. This is just me. My life without prayer is full of discouragement. But when I pray consistently, it keeps me in a momentum of fire, constant happiness, and encouragement. Prayer helps me maintain a momentum of encouragement. It is important to note that you don't need new prayer topics each day before you can pray. You can pray the same topics every day repeatedly or until you get an answer from God. When you pray, always remember to use Biblical scriptures to serve as evidence as to why you believe that God should answer your prayers. When you get a reply from God, it is important that you obey whatever God directs you to do through the Holy Spirit. When you align your prayer requests with your obedience to God's instructions, you provide a conducive atmosphere for God's will to be done.

My most fulfilling prayers are those in which I offered *myself* as the prayer or as an altar to God. I am not asking for anything from Him but just offering myself to Him to make of me what He wants. I end up very transformed. I feel God coming and sitting in my heart, as I fall into deep sleep most of the time. This is the kind of place I would want to be in all my life and in my afterlife.

One great reason I pray is because I want to put my guardian angels to work. I don't want them to be idling and roaming the Heavenly palace. I want them to work for me by fulfilling God's promises in my life. Through my prayer, I am charging up these angels to watch over my destiny and that of my loved ones. My guardian angels are my spiritual police. They help guard me to make sure that I follow the rules that will enable me to enter eternal life.

When I spend time in prayer with God, God gives me wisdom, guidance, direction, and knowledge on how to fix the problems in my life.

Through prayer, God gives me strength to face the challenges that come my way. Personally, I pray because prayer brings me reward. Prayer is one of the ways that I humble myself before God. Prayer and fasting help me get in alignment with God's will in my life. Prayer helps keep my spiritual life in constant lit or ignition with God.

Prayer has four major assignments in the life of a believer.

1. For growth and personal transformation

    Scripture tells us in the Book of Exodus that when Moses came down from Mount Sinai after spending forty days and forty nights with God, his face shone so brightly that Aaron and all the other people were afraid to go near him. After Moses talked to them, only then could they recognize his voice and approach him. They could not reconcile the person they just saw with the Moses they knew because Moses's appearance had been transformed (Exodus 34:2932 ESV).

    Moreover, in the Book of Luke, we see how Jesus took the Apostles Peter, John, and James and went up to the mountain to pray. As He was praying, His facial appearance was altered, and His clothes became dazzling white (Luke 9:29 ESV).

    These scriptures reveal to us that, aside from interceding for others, prayer has a transformative power in the lives of anyone who engages in it. Prayer is one of the bedrocks of personal transformation.

    Personally, whenever I pray, I feel a deeper connection with God and an inner sense of validation and accomplishment. Whenever I pray, I feel a personal intimacy with God and consequently a personal transformation. This personal transformation in turn precedes power demonstration. Nothing changes your inner being like an intimate relationship with God through prayer. When God answers your prayers, you feel loved by Him and even more drawn to Him because you know that He trusts you and your prayers. Prayer has the capacity to transform how you relate with people around you. When you relate with a divine being, it affects how you relate to others. Through prayer, God will do through you, things that you couldn't otherwise do for or by yourself. Prayer connects you to the realm of God and the realm of unlimited possibilities. Prayer can do for you in one minute what you cannot do for yourself in your lifetime.

Mark Batterson said prayer is the difference between the best you can do, and the best God can do. I pray because I want God to change me. When God changes me, he changes my situation. He might not change what I'm currently going through but He's going to change my mindset about what I am going through. This is so I will not look at what I am going through from a victim's perspective. Instead, I will look at it as someone whom God was training by passing her through a firing furnace to be refined for use. Prayer helps me look at my life's challenges from a winner's perspective. Prayer makes me understand that whatever I am going through does not define my future status. Personally, I have noticed that when I abandon my prayer life, I start to develop habits that are not in line with God's promises in my life. Prayer is one of the honest ways of honoring God. Prayer is a form of therapy. Imagine going to a therapist to explain your worries and the counselor gives you coping strategies that you will need to implement in order to adapt to your current situation. Now imagine going to God for therapy and having the Holy Spirit as your counselor instead. That is why the Bible tells us in Matthew 11:28 (ESV), "Come to me all who labor and are heavy laden, and I will give you rest." This is to tell us that there is rest when we confide in God, for God is our ultimate therapist.

2. For making requests and obtaining promises

In the Book of Philippians, we see how Paul tells the Christians not to be anxious and instead, by prayer and supplication, make their requests known to God (Philippians 4:6). This tells us that through prayer, we can make requests to God and obtain His promises. Therefore, prayer serves as a great reward. When we talk about reward, it does not necessarily mean that we will always see or get what we are asking for at that moment. Sometimes, the reward we get for prayer is God's presence. In His presence, we get so much fulfillment that the things of the world do not matter to us. Making prayer a lifestyle by intentionally pursuing the Lord is one of the best ways of obtaining God's promises.

3. For spiritual legislation

The Book of Job 22:28 shows us the power of establishing spiritual legislature through prayer. It says, "Thou shall decree a thing, and it shall be established unto thee. And the light shall shine your ways" (Job 22:28 KJV). This means that through prayer, we can command things to shift in our favor. The last part of this scripture tells us that light shall shine our ways. This means that when we decree a thing, God will give us guidance through His light and the path to achieving this thing will be illuminated by His light. God's light is readily available for us after we set our minds on decreeing whatever we want to see in our lives. The Book of Numbers 14:28 also tells us how God promises His people through Moses that whatever they have spoken to Him, He will certainly do it for them. This shows the power of prayer in the sight of God.

God promises us that whatever we pray about, if it is in alignment with His will in our lives at that time, He will grant us. Didn't Matthew 7:7 tell us the same thing? The Amplified version puts it better. It says, "Ask and keep on asking…seek and keep on seeking…knock and keep on knocking" (Matthew 7:7 AMP). This tells me that prayer should be a constant act or continuous process and not just a one-time thing. Ask God until He becomes tired of you. Imagine praying and asking something from God so much so that when God sees you coming, He says, "Here she comes again or here he comes again. Let me just grant his or her request so that he or she won't keep coming here repeatedly for the same thing." He just grants answers to your requests because he is tired of seeing your face for the same prayer points all the time.

Elijah made a decree through fervent prayer, and it didn't rain for three and a half years. Note that these decrees come to pass if the prayer is fervent. Fervent means having or displaying a passionate intensity. Fervent prayer creates an atmosphere where divinity meets humanity. No wonder James 5:16 (KJV) says,

"The effectual fervent prayer of a righteous man avails much."
Righteousness is obtained only through repentance. That is why
the initial part of this verse says we should confess our sins to one
another. The act of repentance produces righteousness. Attaining
righteousness is a continuous process because, in one way or
another, we are constantly falling short of God's glory.

4. Warfare and intercession

    In the Book of Acts 12, we see how after Herod killed James,
the Jews and Herod arrested Peter and imprisoned him. They
waited to kill him just like James. However, the Christians in the
church prayed earnestly to God for Peter. God sent an angel at
night to unbind Peter and escort him outside the prison. The first
place Peter went was the house where the prayer was taking place.
This chapter tells me that these church members were powerful
intercessors and prayed their warfare prayer at midnight. When
the Christians saw that Herod was ready to do the same thing
to Peter, they leveled up in their prayer and thus Peter's life was
spared. This means that no one was praying and interceding for
James and that was why he was killed. Had the Christians prayed
and interceded for James, maybe God would have spared his
life. This tells us that prayer has a life-saving capacity if taken
seriously. James 5:16 (KJV) says, "The effectual fervent prayer
of a righteous man availeth much." "Effectual fervent" means
prayer done with sincerity and passion. Having faith that God
will grant you answers is a powerful tool to successful answers to
your prayers.

5. Manifestation of the promises of God

    Prayer has the capacity to invoke the promises of God and
bring them to fruition in the lives of His children. Isaiah 41:21
(ESV) says, "Set forth your case, bring your proofs." In other
words, what proof do you have to show that God should bless you?
The proof here is the *Word of God*. That is why during prayer, it is
important to remind God of His promises through His word. For
example, when praying for your children, what proof do you have

that God has promised to bless you and your children? You need to remind God of His promises by quoting scriptures like Isaiah 8:18 (KJV): "I and the children whom the Lord has given me are for signs and wonders." Psalm 127:3 (ESV) says, "Behold, children are a heritage from the Lord, the fruit of the womb a reward." When you quote this during prayer, God Himself will sit in Heaven and say that His son or daughter is presenting a case to Him with evidence. Let our prayers be backed by scriptural evidence before God. By doing so, we are holding God accountable for His promises through His word.

Below are some advantages of what prayer does when we engage in it.

Prayer creates an atmosphere where we trade our;

- sins for God's grace;
- sorrows for God's joy;
- lack for abundance;
- sickness for good health;
- misery for happiness;
- pain for gain;
- weakness for strength;
- doubt for faith;
- fleshly desires for sacrifice;
- greed for generosity
- ordinariness for extraordinariness;
- darkness for light;
- depression for ecstasy;
- poverty for riches;
- barrenness for fruitfulness;
- fear for confidence;
- carelessness for asceticism;
- pride for humility;
- impatience for patience;
- hate for love;
- anxiety for serenity;

- guilt for purity;
- condemnation for plaudit;
- captivity for freedom;
- disgrace for honor;
- ashes for beauty;
- loneliness for companionship;
- orphanhood for parentage;
- mediocrity for excellence;
- death for life;
- being rejected for being chosen;
- incompetence for qualification;
- emptiness for overflowing;
- sadness for laughter;
- ignorance for wisdom:
- shame for fame;
- condemnation for restoration;
- failure for success; and
- rejection for adoption.

Prayer is an atmosphere where you can trade all your worries and be sure to receive a positive transformation from God. Hebrews 7:25 tells us that Jesus is able to save to the uttermost those who draw near to God through Him. He lives to make intercession for them. Whenever we pray, let us learn to invite the Holy Ghost to invade and intoxicate us. Let Her take ownership of our bodies, minds, and souls. Let's permit Her to dwell in us and master our mind and thoughts.

One of the things that stirs up an atmosphere of prayer is *worship*. Whenever I worship, I find myself entering a prayer mood. When you have entered a certain level of spirituality through prayer, you are able to perceive those around you who have attained that same realm. Whenever and wherever you meet one of those people, your spirits connect, and you click with that person. On the other hand, when you meet someone who does not have that spirit or someone who doesn't have a rightful spirit, your spirit will tell you about that person.

I once listened to a woman of God who said that one of her sons brought his girlfriend home to visit them for the first time. She immediately sensed that this girl's spirit was not right, and this girl did not mean well. Nevertheless, this woman welcomed this girl with all love and affection and blessed her with a gift as she departed. As soon as the girl left, this woman sat on the seat where this girl sat and prayed fervently. She commanded that this girl should never return unless she is saved. This girl indeed never returned, and her son never talked about her again. What a story! It is important to note here that this mother didn't chase that girl away in a brutal manner; rather, she showed her love. Even though she saw the evil spirit inhabiting this girl's body, she did not kick her out of her house. If this mother had chased this girl away, it would have opened a portal of accusation that this girl could use against this woman or her son. On the other hand, this woman used wisdom to welcome this girl in the physical but fought the girl in the spiritual. One of the morals of this story is that as Christians, we should be good to everyone but learn to filter or fight people in the spiritual. You can be nice to them yet maintain a distance from them.

Suggested Ways to Maintain Your Prayer Life

Maintaining a life of prayer requires us to put in some work. I am going to share with you some suggested ways that have worked for me. Growing up in my teens, I was very prayerful and buried my heart in Christ. I aspired to become a reverend sister in the Roman Catholic Church. However, I ended up not taking this route as it was not my calling. When I was a middle school student, I used to have ample time to get up early in the morning and go to church even before going to school. As I grew older, my prayer life slowly went downhill because of some lapses in my life. My schedule became busier, and my education became more intense. I struggled with this, especially when I started working full time. I found out that my spiritual life was dropping even more because I couldn't maintain that spiritual fire I had before. During this time, I struggled a lot, and I felt guilty that I wasn't doing what I usually did for God; I didn't spend time with Him like I did before.

However, as time went by, I found ways that helped reactivate that spiritual fire. It is important to know that this is like a cycle. We keep going around and around in our spiritual journeys; there are moments of high tide and moments of low tide. To rekindle my prayer fire, the first thing I did was set aside time to study God's word and to pray. Studying God's word frequently helps me to please God. God's word is more than pixels on a screen. It carries the life-changing power of God. When you study the Bible, you will have dominion. Dominion, in turn, gives you creative and productive power. These creative and productive powers, in turn, give you overcoming power, momentum, expansion capacity, collaboration, monopolization, and globalization, just to name a few. It is important to note that dominion is a mentality. *Dominion* typically refers to control, authority, or power over a particular area, territory, group of people, or domain. It can also indicate sovereignty, supremacy, or rule exercised by a governing entity or individual over a defined jurisdiction. Dominion enables us to think beyond our current situations. The more you read the Bible, meditate on God's Word, and obey God, the more you have the power to overcome the challenges in your life. Reading and meditating on the Word of God helps you to become humble and gives you the power of self-control. The Bible gives you dominion over who you are *not*. Reading and meditating on God's Word helps you overcome thoughts of defeat and depression. Personally, I study the Bible because I want to always have Christ with me, and I want to have strength. I don't want to be weak. Yes, I could be vulnerable in certain circumstances, but I don't want to be weak. Even when I become weak, God, through His Word or through the help of someone he sends to me, will fortify me. I read the Bible because the central message of the Bible is power. It encourages us in our moments of weakness by bringing out our harbored strengths.

Permit me to share with you how I manage my time to ensure I set aside time to study God's Word daily. On days that I do not have to go to work, I study the Bible after dropping the kids off at school. On the days I have to go to work, I will wake up at 5:20 a.m. because I have to leave for work by 6:45 a.m. I will dedicate fifteen minutes studying God's Word and praying before I start getting ready for work. You will think fifteen minutes is a small amount of time but imagine spending this time daily with God. You won't believe how much you will learn if you do this for 365 days. If you ask me if this was easy, I will tell you *no*. This is quite challenging, but doable. Dedicating time for God by waking up fifteen or twenty minutes earlier than your scheduled time is a game changer for your destiny. As time goes by, it will become a part of you so even when you don't set an alarm, you wake up automatically at that time. We have to try to make it a habit to study the Word of God daily. The more you study God's Word and spend time with Him, the more you will hunger to want to read more, know Him more, and implement His words in your daily life. God will be more pleased with you. God's Word helps calm storms of bitterness and revenge in me.

Whenever I read the Bible using my phone, I am easily distracted, especially if I receive any notifications from any social media app. My mind is redirected to the message, and I will feel an urge to check the social media app. Maybe I received a message from a friend or family member. While I'm reading the Word of God, I'll be wondering what the message was all about, especially if I had not heard from that person in a long time. Believe it or not, this distracts your mind from the main focus, which is studying the Word of God. You end up not studying God's Word and not checking the message either, thereby wasting valuable time. I had to fight that by using a hardcopy of the Bible itself as this enabled me to focus more on God's Word. When I read the Bible on my phone, I find myself moving from the Book of Proverbs to the book of Instagram, the book of Facebook, and then the book of TikTok. That is how my attention shifts. Using the hard copy of the Bible helps me maintain that focus on the Word of God without any distractions. I understand carrying a hard copy of the Bible can be frustrating when we have moved into the era of electronics. However, if we have to use our phones, it is advisable to turn off all notifications, so we don't receive them or hear the phone vibrate. If it vibrates, it may cause us not to focus on the Word of God. This is what has actually worked for me.

Now let's talk about some ways that I am using to maintain my prayer life.

1. Finding a local church

I have found that in order to maintain your spiritual or prayer life on constant fire, it is important to go to church every Sunday and/or be in a group in church. Going to church every Sunday, or when you possibly can, helps build your faith, puts you in an environment of constant worship and fellowship with other Christians, and helps you keep the Sabbath, one of the Ten Commandments. Someone once said it does not matter if you go to church or not; church is in your heart. Well, permit me to disagree for once. How stable you are in a particular church plays a great role in the stability of your spiritual life and determines how your spiritual life grows. For me, going to church helps fortify my spirit-person.

There was a period back in 2021 when I was facing a lot of challenges. I went to my local church and the pastor passed out individual virtues to everyone. My virtue was *fortitude* while my husband's was *hospitality*. *Fortitude* means courage in pain and adversity. I was going through a stressful period and that one word changed my perspective. I started not to look at what I was going through as a victim but as someone God was passing through a firing furnace for future refinement. *Fortitude* was the word God was using to tell me that He was with me and that I should stay encouraged. God was using the pastor to tell me to stop asking why but instead to have courage because that was God's will for me at that time. Through fortitude, the Holy Spirit was affirming in my life God's Word according to 1 Thessalonians 5:18 (NIV): "Give thanks in all circumstances; for this is God's will for you in Christ Jesus."

A few years later, I came to see why God made me go through what I was going through. He was delivering me from a major setback. I used the wisdom learned from that experience to help other people in similar situations. Glory, Hallelujah! Imagine that I had not gone to church that day. I would have probably made the wrong decisions, which would have, in turn, landed me in a bad situation. It is usually said that going to church is not a determining factor in making it to Heaven. However, I will add that how stable and participant you are in a Holy Spirit-filled church plays a great role in your relationship with Holy Trinity, your spiritual life, and therefore your chances of making it to Heaven.

2. Secret place with God

Another important thing that helps me maintain my prayer fire is by going to my secret place with God. Everyone has his or her secret place with God. A secret place is the place where you build intimacy with God.

It is the place where you meet divinity or where divinity meets humanity. I don't know about you, but my own secret place with God is fasting. For others, it may be praises, worship, works of charity, visiting the sick, praying for women in labor, caring for widows and orphans, or being involved in the organization committee of a church. Whenever I fast, I discover that my relationship with God becomes stronger, my love for Him increases, and my ability to exercise forgiveness multiplies. Through fasting, God enlightens the eyes of my understanding to see circumstances around me beyond my natural eyes. Most importantly, during or after a fast, God reveals to me His will, either for me, for someone I was praying and interceding for, or even for someone unknown to me. Through fasting, God opens my eyes to see beyond my current situation and directs me what to do in order to stay preserved and protected in moments of droughts, even if these don't make sense to me at the moment. Through fasting, God reveals to me those I have to associate with and those I have to stay away from. My secret place with God is my place of power and divine revelation. Whatever your secret place with God is, it is important to nurture it because therein lies the secret to your destiny and the destiny of those around you. If you do not yet know your secret place with God, examine your life and find the one thing you do that has a positive impact on you or someone else and in turn gives you joy. Then, take it to God in prayer for nurturing. If you don't know what your secret place is, go to God in prayer, ask Him boldly, and He will certainly reveal it to you.

3. Building a prayer altar

Another pertinent thing that has helped me to maintain my prayer fire is by building a prayer altar to God in my home. 2 Chronicles 7:15–16 (GNBDC) says, "I will watch over this Temple and be ready to hear all the prayers that are offered here, because I have chosen it and consecrated it as the place where I will be worshiped forever. I will watch over it and protect it for all time."

What is a prayer altar? A prayer altar is a consecrated place for an encounter between a human and God. It is a system of authorization and a platform where the realm of the heavenly beings makes contact with the physical ground. An altar is a covenant or a place where covenants are made, activated, and maintained. Altars can be physical monuments, institutions, or people. It is a physical portal of entry for angelic visitations. An altar is a pertinent structure in the life of every Christian because it helps maintain your prayer life, which in turn is the most accurate measure of the health of your spiritual life. This prayer altar is a designated area that reminds me that I have made a covenant with God, or I have to spend time with God that day. I placed my altar in a spot where it gets my attention; whenever I walk into or out of my room, I see it. It can be in an area that is very visible and reminds you if you have or have not spent time with God that day. Even when my children, especially my four- and five-year-olds pass by the altar, they know that the altar represents God and they say things like, "in the name of Jesus" or "Good morning (or good afternoon) God." They always say this whenever they come in front of the altar. I firmly believe that this is their own form of prayer. Seeing my kids do this, I can barely contain my delight. I feel really fulfilled knowing that I try my best as a child of God. My kids don't get to say these words in other areas of the house. They say this only when they see the altar.

I remember my son came home from school after his academic awards and placed his honor roll certificate on the altar. When I returned from work, I asked my husband who placed it there and he said our son did. After showing him the certificate, he said he was going to give it to God. These kids see everything we do. This gratifies my soul because my kids grow to know that you can actually have a place in your home that represents God's presence. It is so fulfilling knowing that God is dwelling in that place.

If I pass a day without praying or praying on the altar, passing by or through that altar makes me feel guilty. This altar of God reminds me to constantly be in prayer. When you establish a prayer altar in your home, God will eventually protect your home because your home harbors His altar, His dwelling place. Anyone who comes to your home on a destructive mission or with a spirit contrary to the Holy Spirit would feel uncomfortable and end up leaving even if you do not send the person away. Anyone who comes to your home with good intentions ends up staying and receives a major blessing in return. One of my greatest testimonies about having a prayer altar in my home is that God has answered all of the prayer requests I have made on this altar.

Before building an altar to God in your home, it is important that you first tear down any existing altar that does not glorify God. This is especially true for altars that have been built by us or by our ancestors. You cannot serve two masters at a time. We see a typical example of an altar in Jacob's story (Genesis 28:10 onward). When Jacob was traveling in the desert, he found a place to rest because the journey had been so long and tiring. He decided to lay his head on a stone and rest. As he rested, he dreamed he saw a ladder connecting earth and Heaven on which angels ascended to and descended from Heaven. Jacob's father had built an altar to God on that spot decades earlier. Because nothing was left to mark it as an altar, the area was almost completely bare. What Jacob saw reminded him that his father had built an altar for the Lord there.

Moreover, in 1 Kings 18:36, we see how Elijah approached the altar and prayed. God proved Himself as the *One True God* compared to Baal, the god of the Canaanites. Elijah wanted to prove who the real God was. Elijah and the prophets of Baal had to call on their gods to prove whose god was going to set the altar ablaze without a physical match. When Elijah built an altar that afternoon, he prayed. He called on the God of his forefathers Abraham, Isaac, and Jacob to prove that He was the God of Israel, and that Elijah was God's servant. Elijah begged God to answer him so everyone present would know that He was the Lord God, and that He was bringing his people back to Himself. God answered Elijah's prayer by sending fire, which burned the bulls, stones, water, and all that was placed in the altar. Baal could not set his altar ablaze despite the people cutting themselves and offering their blood as sacrifices.

It is important to note that after building an altar, you have to maintain that altar. How can an altar be maintained so that God's presence does not depart from it? An altar is maintained through repentance, prayer, sacrifice, and offering. It doesn't mean that if you have an altar in your house, your sins are automatically forgiven. No! You must always ask for forgiveness from God for your sins and those of your family. The sacrifices and offerings offered on the altar do not have to be physical gifts. You can give your heart because your heart is the greatest sacrifice. When you give material things to God and your heart is not in or with God, that's not sacrifice. Some forms of offerings that are not physical gifts include singing praises, worshiping, adoration, and intercession. Every now and

39

then, go before the altar of the Most High God to praise and worship God by exalting His holy name and telling Him how good He has been to you and your family and to past generations. Praise and worship provoke God to move mountains and cause chains to be broken. You can also maintain your altar by sowing a seed and by making prophetic decrees and declarations.

4. The YouVersion Bible app

Another method I use to maintain my prayer fire is by using the Bible app called YouVersion. This Bible app that gives you daily scriptures and explanations of these daily scriptures. The authors explain to us how these passages of the day have affected their lives and how they are encouraging us to use it to glorify God. It provides an atmosphere where you can actually spend time with God, reflect on God's Word, and then apply it to any situation in your life. It also gives you a guided prayer in which you can spend four to six minutes praying and reflecting on the word you have just read. Since using this app, I have been able to explore many other aspects. One of the most interesting parts of this app is a feature called "Plans." There, you can find plans depending on what needs to be addressed based on your current circumstance. This section has thousands of write-ups from different authors that we can use to encourage ourselves or others. It has plans for guided prayer and devotion for any kind of circumstance. For example, if I notice that my prayer life is going downhill and I am not praying like I used to, I just type what I want in the "Plans" search bar. Prayers on how to boost my spiritual life will pop up and I will see plans to boost my prayer life. Scriptures encouraging me on how to overcome a particular moment of weakness will appear. For example, I noticed that my first son became a little discouraged in his studies and in other areas of life. I searched for ways to encourage my son in the plans section, and I found interesting scripts and versions that people had written. A typical one I found was "Practical Words for Encouraging Your Son." This is a seven-day devotional that teaches you how to deal with and encourage your son or child. This was very helpful because everything that the daily devotional instructed, I applied to my son, and I saw remarkable changes.

Upon exploring this plans section further, I found several plans written by diverse authors. I found an interesting series called "All Things New" by Kevin Olusola of Pentatonix. This also is a seven-day devotional in which he talks about his battles with stage fright before an audition. These are just a few mentioned plans.

You will always find something depending on what you type in the search bar. Each plan offers unique help. One of the things I have found most useful about this app is the yearly Bible reading plan. Personally, I had always struggled with sticking to my yearly Bible reading plan. But when I stumbled on a plan called "The Bible Recap" by Tara-Leigh Cobble, everything changed for the good. This is one of the most read yearly Bible plans in the YouVersion app. In this plan, Tara assigns Bible chapters to be read daily. She summarizes the chapters and even provides a section for the reader to talk about his or her own interpretation of these chapters. She gives the reader the opportunity to talk about his or her God shot for the day. Tara, through the Holy Spirit, made this Bible reading plan so compelling that after completing each day's reading, I anticipate the next day's reading. Since following this plan, I have tried not to miss reading the Bible a single day. Even if I missed any day, I could always come back to it. This is so fulfilling. Several other plans are available to help encourage Christians in various areas of their lives. I challenge you to explore this app like I am doing. This app has blessed me a great deal in diverse ways and continues to bless me. I believe it will do the same for you in Jesus's name. Amen.

Let's explore a little history about the Bible app YouVersion.

Craig Groeschel, the founder and pastor of Life.Church, was interviewed Bobby Grunwald, founder of YouVersion, in one of his leadership podcasts. Bobby talked about how the idea of creating the Bible app came about. He said the whole idea came when he was at an airport in Chicago in 2006. As he was waiting in the queue, he began imagining creating an app that would enable him and others to study the Word of God in any place they find themselves. He thought how he could read the Bible anywhere he finds himself without necessarily carrying the hard copy around. He mentioned how he has struggled to consistently read the Bible and maintain his prayer life even when he was at home. Traveling made it more difficult for him to read the Bible. While waiting in line, he envisioned consistently reading the Bible, even when he was not in possession of the hard copy. He also thought about creating a website containing the Bible for easy access and praying. It started with a problem, which produced the idea on how to solve the problem.

He also talked about how he did not have any resources to start the app. However, he and his team started a website in early 2007 and launched it in September 2007. This website idea ended up being a total failure. They had planned to shut it down in 2008. Before shutting it down, however, they decided to evaluate why it failed. In the process of evaluating it, they noticed they had created this website for use on a computer while many people at that time used their Blackberry phones and other smartphones more during the day. They came up with the idea of redesigning the website so it could be visible on a Blackberry phone or any kind of smartphone. That way, people using their smartphones during the day would be able to use the app. That is how YouVersion came into existence. When Apple decided to launch an app store, Bobby and his team found a nineteen-year-old boy who helped them build the YouVersion app for the iPhone store. They then applied for approval from Apple. As soon as they submitted their application, Apple approved it. The YouVersion app was among the top 200 free apps on the store within three days of its launch. At the start, 83,000 people downloaded the app. These people opened the app multiple times a day, as indicated by their app analytics. Bobby and his team were so astonished. Today, his team has thirty-five employees and over one thousand volunteers. Initially, YouVersion was just in two languages. Over the years, people all over the world started requesting translated versions. Bobby and his team worked hard again and, through the support of partnerships and sponsorships, were able to make YouVersion available in over 1200 languages, ensuring they could offer the Bible to every single person in the language he or she understood.

Today, over six million people have the app installed on their devices. The app is influencing people all over the world in every sphere of their lives, ranging from arts and entertainment to business, education, family, government, media, and religion. Based on the analytics of this app, over seventy billion Bible chapters have been read, twelve billion audio chapters have been listened to, and four billion highlights have been bookmarked.

In addition, 2.4 billion plans have been completed, 330 million people have installed the app, 950 million verses have been shared, and 27 million friends have been connected.[3] These statistics are from ten years ago.

Bobby and his team came up with another Bible app called Bible Lens. With this app, you will be able to take a picture of an object and submit it to this app. The app will bring up a biblical scripture talking about that object. For example, if you took a picture of a wedding ring, the app would bring up scriptures about marriage. It will bring up scriptures on how to live with your spouse and other issues. This started because Bob had an idea and identified a problem. He tried to find a solution to the problem. This led to one development after another. Bobby declared that when he and his team started this, they did not know what God was about to do, but God exceeded their expectations. This story of the birth of the YouVersion app has encouraged me, and I hope it also encourages you. What is that difficult situation that you're going through? You have probably tried everything within your power and explored all the options, but you think there is no solution. Think about Bobby. If he had shut down the website after its initial failure and agreed that there was no solution, YouVersion wouldn't have been born. Today, Bobby and all of us are able to read the Bible in places we have never been before using our smartphones.

I would like for us to use Bobby's story as encouragement and to remind us not to give up despite what we are facing right now. Maybe you have been meaning to start a business, go to school even though you think you are too old, or to write a book. You keep feeling that you cannot do it, just like me. I want to encourage you that there is no better time than now. Just like Bobby, we will need the help of a team or other people to help boost our ideas and give us suggestions to make our plans come to fruition. The Bible says in Ecclesiastes 4:9 (GNBDC), "Two are better than one, because together they can work more efficiently." The King James Version makes it sound even better: "Two are better than one: because they have good reward for their labor." The only thing we will need to do is to pray to God to show us the right people to work with so that our projects will be successful. Remember, Bob said they had no resources in

---

[3] Craig Groeschel, "Q&A with YouVersion Founder Bobby Gruenewald and Craig Groeschel," YouTube, 21:25. July 31, 2018, https://www.youtube.com/watch?v=1fxPn1JVyks.

the beginning. They just came up with ideas. He found that he could not afford to pay the engineers in Silicon Valley to develop the app. He made use of the resources available near him and one of the main resources was this nineteen-year-old boy who was into technology. This boy was able to create this app. Think about it: Bobby, who was more advanced in age and had presumably more wisdom than this nineteen-year-old, could not create this app. However, this boy of nineteen created it. I want this story to encourage us that God can use anyone to help us, no matter how small we may think they are. Think about the story of the maid in the Bible who had the solution to Narman's leprosy. Though she was just a maid, she had a solution that helped him.

5. Family devotions

Another method I use to maintain my spiritual life is through daily family devotions. You can use any devotional book from your church. The one I use I have been using for the past ten years. This book has been so helpful in directing my spiritual path and how I live with my family. It directs me on how to maintain my prayer fire, how to be a better wife, how to raise my kids, how to maintain my overall relationships, and so many other good aspects in my Christian journey. Family devotion is very important. You can have it either in the morning or in the evening depending on what works for your family. For my family, we prefer to have it in the evenings because in the morning, we are all in a hurry to go to school or to work and we do not want to pray in a rush. When we all are back home, we have more time to read the Bible and pray.

I know there are many ways out there you can use to maintain your prayer fire. However, these have been the most effective for me.

CHAPTER 4

VISION BOARD

A vision is the GPS of your dreams.[4]
—Terri Savelle Foy

Arnold Schwarzenegger once said, "Create a vision of who you want to be and then leave that picture as if it were already true."[5] This statement from Schwarzenegger brings us to the simplest definition of a vision board. A vision board is a desired picture of the future, a picture of how you want your future to be or to look like. It is a picture of where you want to find yourself in the near or far future. It's what you want to achieve or overcome in the future despite your current circumstances. To me, a vision is a list of sanctified imaginations. Making a vision of yourself in the future puts you in a position of expectation: what you expect of yourself as you align yourself with the promises of God. Having a vision enables you to make the necessary adjustments in your current mindset, perception, and activities to match your future expectations or visions.

---

[4] Terri Savelle Foy, "Unlocking Your Dreams, Best Vision Board Compilation," YouTube, 47:37, December 2023, https://www.youtube.com/watch?v=CvYQtqZnBw0.
[5] Arnold Schwarzenegger, "Create a vision of who you want to be, and then live into that picture as if it were already true," AZ Quotes, accessed November 5, 2024, https://www.azquotes.com/quote/835670#google_vignette.

Those who know me and have had the opportunity to be around me will tell you that I am a very optimistic person. I'm always working on a new project or aiming to achieve something new, no matter how small it may be. One time, I pleaded with a friend and coworker to reference me for a job I was applying for. One of the reference questions asked her to talk about my weaknesses. She said, "Nicole is an overachiever, and she believes she can do anything." She told me how her husband laughed when she showed him this. This may seem funny to see your friend write that your strongest weakness is that you are an overachiever. Many people say I am an overachiever, but few people have asked me what drives me to be that way. The scripture says, "Ask the Lord to bless your plans, and you will be successful in carrying them out" (Proverbs 16:3 GNBDC). This verse means you must have plans. You cannot just sit around idling and expect God to tell you everything you need to do. Scripture says God has given us sound minds to make critical thinking decisions. The Amplified version puts this even better.

> For God did not give us a spirit of timidity or cowardice or fear, but [He has given us a spirit] of power and of love and of sound judgment and personal discipline [abilities that result in a calm, well-balanced mind and self-control]. (2 Timothy 1:7 AMP)

Permit me to emphasize the words "sound judgment" and "well-balanced mind." Since we have minds that are well-balanced and have sound judgment, it means we can make concrete plans, present them to God, and ask Him to bless them. We can also ask Him if these plans are in alignment with His will for us. God will bless them even if those plans don't materialize at that moment. Nevertheless, the grace to succeed in them has already been released. Now, the success of those plans will depend on whether that is the will of God for you at that time. I make plans at the beginning of each year for things I would like to achieve in the coming year. I strongly believe that the thoughts and visions you build in your heart will shape the way your life goes.

That is why it is important to have a vision of your own life and how you want it to be. You can do this by creating a vision board where you write down what you want to achieve or what you want to be. I use a vision board to help direct my path and encourage my soul. If we read Habakkuk 2:2, it says, "Then the Lord answered me and said, 'Write the vision and engrave it plainly on [clay] tablets so that the one who reads it will run.'" This verse is so encouraging because it tells us how God is instructing us to write a vision of what we want to do. We make it plain so that anyone who passes across it is able to read it and be encouraged. A vision board works best for those who operate by faith not those who operate by sight. If you operate by sight, then your vision will be limited only to what you see. If you don't know what vision to write, then go to God and ask Him. James 4: 3 NIV says, "You do not have because you do not ask God." Most people do not have the life they dream because they do not ask for this life from God. Jabez looked at his life, desired a change, cried out to God, and guess what? God changed his name.

Writing a vision places you at a higher level of thinking. When writing these visions, be clear and be specific; don't be vague. I challenge you to write down everything you want from God on a piece of paper or on your phone. You cannot let the visions remain just in your head. As you have envisioned it, write it down. Write down everything, no matter how trivial you think it may be. Read it to yourself every morning when you wake up and every night before going to bed. Put pictures of it as your screensaver. Post a picture of it everywhere around you, making sure it is visible only to you because a vision board is personal. Speak to your visions and dreams and command them to come to fruition. Be about your vision board. Then, start taking action to implement what it takes to achieve all what you've written down. Every third quarter or so, reassess your list and write down all you have achieved. Find out why you failed to achieve what you did not. If you did all these in faith and expectation in God, I assure you that you will be amazed by your results.

It is important to note that there will always be voices in your head telling you that these visions are absurd and will never come to pass, that those visions are too big and there is no way you will be able to achieve them. Your faith alone is able to silence these voices. Do not let these voices compel you to reduce or shrink your vision. Rather, what you need to do is to enlarge your faith. Most importantly, sow a seed to your vision. Make a memorable offering to God about your seed. For example, if you believe in God for a baby, sow a seed in the lives of orphans or single, struggling mothers. Even if all the items on your list did not come to fruition at your set time, just remember Habakkuk 2:3 (KJV): "For the vision is yet for an appointed time, but at the end it shall speak, and not lie: though it tarry, wait for it; because it will surely come, it will not tarry." Did you get that? Scripture tells us that even if we do not achieve everything on our lists at the set time, we should wait for it with anticipation for it will come to pass at the appointed time. Then, we praise God before these visions manifest. Believe that the dreams have already come to pass. One of the highest expressions of faith is when you praise God before something you are believing Him for happens.

In writing your visions, make your dreams so big that the only way of achieving them is by using your faith. When you ask big, believe it and it will be yours. Dream big and send God the bill. If this is within His will for you at that time, He will answer you. He is the God of abundance, and He can afford it. When you ask big, God will validate His word. I can back this up with scriptures: "Therefore I tell you, whatever you ask in prayer, believe that you have received it, and it will be yours" (Mark 11:24 ESV). Don't ask God something from a poverty mentality but rather from an abundant mentality because God is the God of abundance. One of the major ways in which you build your faith in your vision is through the Word of God. Embed your visions in the Word of God and in the promises of God. Be bold enough to ask something big from God. Steve Harvey said his mother engraved seven words in his heart and these words have taken him to places he never could have imagined. These words are "You have not because you ask not." He says he was not living the life he wanted because he wasn't asking that life from God. When he began asking for the kind of life he wanted, God surpassed his expectations. Whatever you want to see happen in your life tomorrow or the future, ask God for it today. The Gospel of John 14:14 (ESV) says, "If you ask me anything in my name, I will do it."

In the first chapter of the Book of Revelations, we see how the Apostle John was sent to prison on an island called Patmos because he preached the Word of God and the testimony of Jesus. We see how Jesus appeared to him and said, "Write therefore the things that you have seen, those that are and those that are to take place after this" (Revelation 1:19 ESV). Paul was to write all that Jesus had shown him so he could take them to the seven churches in Asia undergoing persecutions and tribulations. In the same way, when things are not going the way you want in your life, write down what you want to see. If you are going through financial hardship, write financial abundance; for lack of the fruits of the womb, put down twins or triplets. These are just a few. Write down all that you want to see happen in your life. Believe in what you have written while trusting God to guide you as you believe that these written things will come to fruition. Having a vision for yourself puts you in a place of discipline and with discipline comes wisdom. With discipline, you calculate and critically think before making any move. This is wisdom.

The Bible also tells us in Proverbs 19:8 (GNBDC), "Do yourself a favor and learn all you can; then remember what you learn, and you will prosper." By writing down your visions, you are setting yourself up to be open to learning new things. To achieve some of your goals, you need to learn the skills necessary to achieve these goals. Only after learning these skills will, you achieve these goals and prosper in that area of your life. The number one predictor that your visions will be successful is when you are intentional about them. Be intentional about taking the necessary steps that will pave a way for the success of your dreams. Document what you are learning and the areas you are growing up in. Get yourself and the things around you organized and focused. One important fact to note here is that these visions are not found *ahead* of you rather *inside* of you. That is why they are your visions, and they are unique to you alone. You use the ideas inside of you, combined with the resources around you, to get what is ahead of you. You write these visions based on the needs you have or of the things you want to become or see your life turn into.

At the start of each year, write your visions or what some people call your resolutions. What resolutions or visions do you have for yourself for that year? At the end of that year, where do you want to see yourself? What plans do you have? What do you want to accomplish for that year? A good plan today is better than a perfect plan tomorrow.

With a vision board, you can set your goals for that year. Once you have set those goals, you put yourself in an organized position that will enable you to work in order to achieve those goals. That is how I try to set myself up for the next coming year.

A vision board is important because it allows you to frame your future. It permits you to focus on where you are going. It can be likened to the GPS of your future. It's like the GPS of your dreams. God's Word says that where there is no vision, His people perish (see Proverbs 29:18 KJV). This means that anyone without a vision has a higher chance of perishing. Perishing doesn't necessarily mean that you die physically. Rather, you won't be able to live the fulfilled life that God has called you to live. A vision will serve as a roadmap toward fulfilling your destiny.

Your vision board can be either in digital or paper form, depending on the resources you have available. In the past, I have always used paper to write whatever I want to accomplish. With the coming of smartphones, I found it very easy to create my vision board. There are YouTube videos that teach you a step-by-step process on how to create your vision board. One of these videos is by Marivon Sama and entitled "How to create a digital vision board in five minutes." In this video, she walks you through the step-by-step process of creating one in the shortest possible time using Canva. This tool is really practical, and I could easily use it to make my digital vision board using my phone. I know there are so many other videos out there to help you create your vision board. Go with what works best for you.

In her book *Hello, Tomorrow!: The Transformational Power of Vision*, Dr. Cindy Trimm explains in detail the importance of vision boards and how they have helped her become the person she is today.[6] f she can attest to the importance of visions and how they have helped her, so can we.

Since I am an overachiever, according to my friend, I write my vision for that year and for the upcoming five or ten years. By doing this, I envision the legacy that I want to leave for generations to come. You can do this by writing down your short-term or yearly visions and long-term visions for generations to come. It is important to note that after you write your visions, life may or may not always go as planned. You can always readjust or modify these visions as time goes on. For my yearly vision, I

---

[6] Cindy Trimm, *Hello, Tomorrow!: The Transformational Power of Vision* (Lake Mary, FL: Charisma, 2018), chapter 10.

write down what I want to accomplish for that year. I make sure these are physical things that I can actually accomplish, not just random things. For example, you cannot randomly write that you will take a trip to the moon because lunar tourism is not yet possible. However, you can write that you start saving money toward acquiring a property on planet Earth. What you think you can accomplish and what you think God can help you accomplish that year is very important. Do not write too many big plans that you cannot accomplish, like the example of visiting the moon. You might end up being very discouraged. Write things that you can accomplish and that are possible and feasible. Your vision can be *big yet possible*. In addition, create a generational long-term goal or generational vision board that will help you create wealth or generational wealth for your family to enjoy even when you are no longer alive. Set this goal even if you do not have any capital now. This is a typical application of faith. Hebrews 11:1 (KJV) says, "Now faith is the substance of things hoped for, the evidence of things not seen." For your vision to work, you must have faith that God will give you the grace to achieve them in the best possible ways and at their rightful seasons. Faith is more than just checking a mental box. Rather, it is the firm belief that God will help you accomplish them. Your faith in God about the success of your vision alone is able to stir up an atmosphere of success and materialization of your plans.

One of the topics on my vision board for 2023 was that I was going to read one hundred books. Practically speaking, this was almost impossible for me to accomplish considering my busy schedule. After doing some research, I discovered that I could achieve this goal by listening to the audiobooks because I am not a fast reader. I am a methodical reader; when I read, I want to be able to synthesize every line appropriately and this takes a lot of time. It is important to note that even with this goal of using audiobooks instead, I had to set strategies to enable me to accomplish it. I took one hundred and divided it by fifty-two weeks, which is the number of weeks in a year. This placed me at approximately two books per week or approximately eight to nine books per month. Because of my work, family, and other life issues, I challenged myself by taking a higher level of performance by adjusting the audiobooks' narrative speed. On audiobooks, you can increase the narrative speed; it ranges from 0.5 times to 3.5 times. I usually listen at the rate of 1.3 times normal speed using my ear pods. There is also a timer you can set for how long you want to listen to those audiobooks. As I listen to these books, I pause, and I write down important points or any points that catch my attention.

I recommend that you read *The 12-Week Year* by Brian Moran and Michael Lennington. This book teaches you how to chunk your year into three separate months, which the author calls the twelve-week year. This plan enables you to write a vision board for what you want to accomplish in the first three months of the year from January through March. This is very important because it helps you set specific and measurable goals. Stating them positively, creating a realistic stretch, and assigning accountability makes you time bound. This will enable you to write down your goals and set priority to the ones that have the greatest impact. Write down what you want to accomplish for each week, taking into consideration that life happens. Do your best to figure out how you can overcome obstacles. Build your plan around what is most important in your life and the support structure you need to put in place to make this work for you. Always make sure that you measure your plans because measurement drives the execution process. Even if you do not accomplish the goals of a certain week, do not become discouraged because some weeks are not the same. Life happens. Learning to spend your time intentionally is a very important step in achieving your set goals. Never let excuses get into your way of creating your goal. If you did not accomplish the goals of a particular week, make the decision to never be a victim again. Let these decisions be grounded in Christ. Sometimes, achieving your goals involves a series of trials and errors and even failures. The good thing about failure is the experience or lesson you gain from it. That is why some people say show me a person who has made many errors in life, and I will show you a person with wisdom because mistakes give you wisdom.

It is important to know that when you write your visions, you must be intentional about them. You don't have to let yourself give up on them easily at the slightest doubt or chance of failure. Intentionality and action is going to bring your visions and ideas to fruition. Intentionality is the precursor to innovation and resourcefulness. Intentionality forces you to have breakthrough ideas in the most challenging situations of your vision. Intentionality blinds you to the lack of abilities, intellect, and resources you need to achieve these visions. Intentionality forces you to operate by faith and not by sight. Vision involves risks, which means you must be ready to take leaps of faith. The degree of intentionality that you have toward your vision will act as a catalyst to accomplishing these visions. Through your visions, you are designing your destiny in disguise. That is why you must be optimistic about your visions.

One of the secret ingredients to the success of your visions is *positivity*. You need to have faith that things are going to work even if everything seems obscured at that moment. Dr. Cindy Trimm once said, "The most expensive real estate in the world is the human mind."[7] This is true because the mind has the ability to generate an idea until it comes to fruition. I believe that whenever you set the intention to do something, Heaven will obligate itself to provide you with the necessary resources to bring those dreams to fruition. What you think, write down, and then implement the necessary actions to bring that idea to reality and a great innovation will be born. This was how great scientists like Albert Einstein and Thomas Edison birthed the theory of general relativity and the light bulb respectively. When you have written those visions, don't wish for fewer obstacles; rather, wish for more skills to overcome any obstacles that come your way. The secret to the success of your vision is hidden in your daily routine. The little things you do daily affect how and when you will achieve your dreams. It's what you do daily that adds up.

Vision plus prayer plus faith plus discipline plus action leads to success. Discipline is the bridge between your vision and your destiny.

Let me share with you an example of a vision I wrote for myself ten years ago right before I was about to get married.

Vision Number 1: I wrote and prayed that I wanted the Lord to bless me with four children as the fruits of my marriage by the tenth year of my marriage.

Action Number 1: I made four tiers of my wedding cake to represent the four children I planned to have.

Faith Number 1: I prayed earnestly for myself and for other women seeking for the fruit of the womb and believed that God had answered my prayers

---

[7] Trimm Cindy. "Next-Level Thinking [The Power of Intention] Dr. Cindy Trimm" YouTube, 1:03:19. July 14, 2022. https://youtu.be/xiuTM0r6YiU?si=8SPUa5NXPKX0LsMg.

Faith Number 2: After having my first child and moving to the United States to join my husband, I bought a pregnancy test kit with three kits inside to represent the three more kids I was expecting from God.

Success Number 1: The Lord blessed me with my first son exactly nine months after my wedding.

Success Number 2: By the seventh year of my marriage, I was carrying my fourth child to the glory of God.

Obstacle faced: My second pregnancy was a miscarriage, but God blessed me with my daughter a month after this miscarriage.

The moral of this analysis is that I had a vision for my marriage, presented it to God for blessing, had faith that He would grant it, interceded for other women who were seeking the fruit of the womb, faced obstacles and overcame them, and the Lord granted my request. I remember how each time a friend of mine who was struggling to get pregnant called me to help pray for her to conceive, I would pray for and with her. Whenever I prayed, the Lord would answer our prayers by blessing them and me with a child. That is part of the reason why my last two children were not planned. Left to me and my husband, we would have waited a little longer before conceiving our third and fourth children. They both came as a surprise to us. We had no choice but to accept it as the will of God.

In the course of seven years of my marriage, three of my friends who unexpectedly became pregnant and did not want to keep the pregnancy came to me requesting I recommend medications to terminate their pregnancies. I am a nurse, and they believed I knew the abortion medications. After preaching and advising them about the importance of not indulging in such an act, I succeeded in convincing two of them. They gave birth to their babies. When they had these babies, they called me and thanked me for giving them such good advice. These babies changed the trajectory of their lives for good. One of the ladies was very promiscuous and this baby changed the trajectory of her life. She went back to school and is now a successful teacher living a beautiful life in Christ while raising her daughter.

The other lady had a son, and the arrival of this boy opened doors of opportunities for her and her boyfriend. They got married. She became a professional baker and owned her own successful bakery and pastry shop. Now, the third lady, who did not heed my advice, proceeded to have an abortion. I called her several times, but she wouldn't take my calls. Though she didn't take my calls, she went to three of our friends telling them how bad I was and all sorts of lies about me. Prior to this, an angel of God came to me telling me to stay away from this lady and that I shouldn't allow her to be close to me ever again. About a week later, all three friends she complained to about me called me telling me what she had said about me. When I told them what had transpired, they were so downcast to see how much hatred this lady had toward me for giving her such great advice. To this day, this lady has never had a baby and is still bitter toward me. Another friend of ours told me all the lies she keeps saying about me. Honestly, I hold no grudge against her. All I know is that I did my part, and I leave God to be her judge.

Over time, I have noticed that the devil can test you with situations of compromise about one or more of your visions. However, if you stick to the authenticity of your vision, your faith in God, and your dependence on God for guidance, God will certainly help you not to compromise like the devil wants you to. Most often, these situations of compromise appear to be very sorrowful, compelling you to want to give into the temptation. You should have seen the way these three ladies came crying to me. They expressed desperation about how these pregnancies were going to ruin the trust their families had in them and consequently their lives. I strongly believe that God blessed me with the set number of children I had requested from Him because I did not encourage these ladies to commit abortion. In addition, I was always praying for other women who were also seeking for the fruit of the womb.

It is important to note that pursuing the path to achieving your visions comes with a lot of sacrifices. The journey toward achieving your visions can be very arduous. Nevertheless, with faith and persistence, you can achieve them. On the night Dr. Martin Luther King Jr. was assassinated, he was going to deliver a speech in Memphis, Tennessee. In his pocket was a copy of the speech he was to deliver. An important message of his speech emphasized that *nothing is gained without sacrifice*. This means that he was the sacrifice so the blacks of this nation could have the opportunities they now have today. Though he is not alive today, the dreams he had and fought for are now manifesting in this generation. Like Dr. King, let's be ready to engage in sacrificing many things (not our lives, of course), especially the things that distract us, so that our visions will be achieved.

CHAPTER 5

THE SPIRIT OF DISCERNMENT

> A person's thoughts are like water in a deep well, but
> someone with insight can draw them out.
> —Proverbs 20:5 (GNBDC)

The spirit of discernment is a gift of the Holy Spirit. This gift of discernment makes you very shrewd. To be shrewd means to have or show sharp powers of judgment. It makes you very quick to observe. Discernment is the ability to perceive and understand things clearly, often with a keen insight or intuition. It is a superior faculty of spiritual perception. It involves the process of distinguishing between right and wrong, truth and falsehood, or making sound judgments about complex situations. It is the ability to distinguish between what God is doing from what the devil is doing. Discernment typically relies on careful observation, critical thinking, wisdom, and sometimes spiritual or intuitive guidance. It is an important skill in various aspects of life, including decision making, problem solving, and ethical reasoning. People often cultivate discernment through experience, reflection, and learning.

Spiritually speaking, one of the criteria for measuring the maturity of a believer is through the strength of his or her discernment. Hebrews 5:14 (ESV) says, "But solid food is for the mature, for those who have their powers of discernment trained by constant practice to distinguish good from evil." We are living in a very spiritual world. In order to continuously live as believers, we need to train and sharpen our spirit of discernment. As believers, we can avoid many troubles if we practice discernment. The spirit of discernment creates an awareness of God's will concerning issues happening to or around us. It enables us to make decisions that are in alignment with the will of God. Most often, these decisions are the most uncomfortable decisions to make, but you must make them if you want to remain within the atmosphere of God's will. Through the spirit of discernment, God is able to reveal things that are about to happen. When He reveals these things, that is because His power has gone ahead to overcome them.

One operation of the spirit of discernment in the life of a believer can be the difference between victory and defeat in that believer's life. Meanwhile, the lack of discernment can sometimes cost you your life or something very dear to you. The spirit of discernment prevents you from making careless destiny decisions. The spirit of discernment sharpens your wisdom, which in turn directs your life. The spirit of discernment provides the ability to disrupt the plans you have for your life since these plans may not be the will of God. The spirit of discernment will help you know who to keep as friends and who to stay away from. Once you have trained your spirit of discernment, it is important to respect and obey the impulses that come from it. For example, you may plan to go on a journey, but through the spirit of discernment, the Holy Spirit instructs you not to step out and you obey. Later, you receive the news that a major accident happened to those who took that journey. In this case, your discernment has saved you from untimely death. The spirit of discernment is able to recognize jealous demons that disguise themselves as supportive angels.

In 1 Corinthians 12:10 (KJV), we read that one person may receive the ability of "the working of miracles; to another prophecy; to another descending of spirits; to another diverse kinds of tongues; to another the interpretation of tongues." The spirit of discernment entails understanding or knowing something through the power of the Holy Spirit. It involves the ability to know what the Holy Spirit is saying. It includes perceiving the true character of people, and the source and meaning of spiritual manifestations. When you have the gift of discernment, you are able to detect the arrows and hidden evil in people. You are also able to detect your arrows and the evil that is concealed in you. It helps you to find and bring forth the good that may be concealed in others. Most often when the devil uses someone to condemn an innocent person and has all the evidence that can be used against that innocent person, only a person with the spirit of discernment can recognize that this person is innocent. The spirit of discernment enlightens your understanding, so you don't judge things with your natural eyes but see the truth hidden in them. Someone with the spirit of discernment has great insight and is able to draw out the deep thoughts or sense the evil of those around them.

Personally, I will advise every Christian to pray for the gift of the spirit of discernment. I ask that the Lord open and enlighten the eyes of our understanding so we will never misjudge people based on what others say about them. I pray that the Lord God will give us wisdom to detect and depict the evil hidden in others, their evil intentions, and the hidden evil arrows in people. Then we will be able to understand the true character of people and the source and meaning of spiritual manifestations.

In my walk with God, I have come to understand that the spirit of discernment in my life becomes more readily available to me the more I stay grounded in Christ and in the Word of God, and when I intercede for people. Through intercession, God is able to grant me access and trust me with the secrets He has over people and over territories. Intercession grants me access to illumination and understanding about what is hidden in the dark. Then, I will be able to understand the real meaning, intentions, and characters of people around my life or people far away. Intercession is a seed that sharpens your walk with Christ because Christ Himself is our intercessor in Heaven. As stated in Romans, "Jesus, who is at the right hand of God, who indeed is interceding for us" (Romans 8:34 ESV).

In Job chapter 42:10, we see how the Lord turned the captivity of Job when he prayed for his friends. The Lord gave Job twice as much as he had before. This means that when you pray for your friends, families, people, and territories, the Lord hears the prayers and in turn answers your personal prayers. When you pray and intercede for people, the Lord is already granting answers to your personal prayers or needs. Intercession is an important tool you do not want to skip or neglect in your walk with God.

As I was growing up, I had the urge to pray for women who are seeking the fruit of the womb. As far back as the age of eleven, during my prayer time, I found myself praying for God to bless women who wanted to have children. That is how I kept praying as I was growing up and how I pray to this day. Whenever I was about to start praying, the first thing that came to my mind was to pray for women wanting children or for pregnant women. I have kept this topic on my prayer list for the longest possible time. Because I opened up the heavenly portal, that channel of praying for women seeking the fruit of the womb, I realized that God always places around me women who either want to have children or who are pregnant. For example, back in my university days, most often at night, I would jump out of my bed from a dream because the Lord gave me the name of someone to wake up and pray for. The Lord will instruct me to pray for this or that person because she is seeking the fruit of the womb.

I remember one particular night when the Lord woke me up and told me to pray for a former coworker who had several miscarriages. I woke up, prayed for her, and then went back to sleep. The following morning when I went to church, I saw that person and immediately remembered the incident from the night. I told her about what happened. I noticed how she and her husband froze in a stare as they both looked at me because this was one of their top secrets. I never saw her again after that. One year later, I met another coworker with whom we had all worked. This coworker told me that the other coworker had a baby boy. I praised God for His constant and immeasurable love. My heart leaped for joy as I glorified God. The coworker I met was surprised at how happy I was and never understood the reason for such happiness. Only God and I knew what He had done. I have never set eyes on that coworker again, but I know that she and her babies are in good health.

In another scenario, I used to rent a house where the bedroom window was next to a maternity clinic. Most often when women were in labor, their families would come and pray for safe delivery next to my bedroom window. I just found myself waking up and joining them in prayer. We prayed until they received news that the woman had given birth or until they stopped praying.

Because I kept praying for these women, God kept sending me women who wanted to have children. He called them by name and asked that I pray for them, and I obeyed. I remember one time when the Lord asked me to pray for one of my friends. She had been married for about five years and so desperately wanted children, she was about to go into depression. I realized I had not heard from this friend for a very long time. I obeyed and prayed for her. Nine months later, her husband posted the picture of their newborn on Facebook, and I blessed God for them. Many other scenarios arose when God requested that I pray for women and months later, I found them pregnant or carrying their babies. What a joy!

You will think that because I was praying for these women that my pregnancy or child-bearing journey would have been a smooth one. You will be shocked! When it was my turn to have my own babies, I had the scariest attacks whenever I was pregnant. Though I came out victorious each time and my babies and I were in good health, it was always a challenge. In each pregnancy, the devil tried to seize the opportunity to harm me and my baby so I would accuse God. In each situation, God showed Himself as mighty in battle.

Let me share with you all my child-bearing story of how the devil sought to attack me for praying for all these women, and how God delivered me every time.

When I got married, my husband and I prayed and asked God to bless us with a child. I conceived on my wedding night. Three months into this pregnancy, my mom was diagnosed with leukemia. The financial responsibilities, the poor medical interventions in a third-world country, the trauma of seeing my mom suffer and knowing that she might soon be dead, coupled with the challenges of being a first-time mom felt very frustrating. I suffered a lot of betrayal from my friends, family, siblings, in-laws, coworkers, and even the landlord of the home I was living in. I felt like the devil turned the whole world against me. The attacks were enormous, but each time I wanted to worry, God gave me inner peace. Most often when I slept at night, I would feel God's presence in my bedroom.

When I was about seven months pregnant, I was asleep one night and turned in bed. I found an angel standing as a guard next to my bedroom door. I went back to sleep feeling so at peace and slept soundly. This went on until it was time for me to have my baby. My mum, being in an incapacitated state, advised me that I should take her kid sister, a mother of five who happened to be in the same city as me, with me for the delivery. It is advisable that a new mom has her baby alongside another experienced mom. I felt comfortable with this because I babysat my aunt's last child four years prior when she had the baby. Early one morning, a friend of mine who also happened to be one of my prayer partners called me and said she had a dream that I was on my way to have a baby, and that God said He would be with me. I pondered over what could be awaiting me in the delivery room. Later on, I woke up to have breakfast and went back to bed. About four hours later, around noon, my water broke. Immediately after this happened, a dark cloud filled the sky, and it rained heavily for about fifteen minutes. After that, the sun came out and shone so brightly. I remember one of my sisters said this indicated that the arrival of my baby meant a lot in the spirit realm. I paid little attention as I was anxious about the slight contractions I had started feeling. I packed my valise to head to the hospital.

Upon arrival at the hospital, I had dilated to three centimeters according to the midwife's examination. The doctor said they should give time for labor to come naturally since I was a primigravida. By morning, I had dilated to six centimeters with the aid of Pitocin. I was given the maximum dose of Pitocin. The contractions intensified with no further dilation. I stayed at six centimeters for eleven hours until the doctor consented to a C-section. With all the pain, tiredness, and hunger, I agreed to this surgery just to have everything done with. Then, I turned and saw the picture of Jesus on the wall. I remembered that God had promised me I would deliver this baby like a Hebrew woman. I asked myself, *How is it that I prayed for women and now that it's my turn, I have this difficulty? Why am I accepting this surgery when this is not how the Lord told me I would have this baby?* Then, I cried out to God, begging Him to open His book of remembrance and come defend His word as He had promised. A coworker of mine came and prayed with me. I remember praying to the point where the contractions stopped. I ended my prayer with Psalm 91. The delivery team joined me in prayer by worshiping God with songs. At the end of our prayers, the doctor asked to examine me. I had dilated to nine and a half centimeters, just half an inch short of the required dilation. I remember the OBGYN doctor telling me he was going to take me to the delivery bed and that I needed to work with him to safely deliver this baby. That was how my baby was born to the glory of God. When the baby was born, the whole team shouted, "Victoire," the French word for victory.

Meanwhile, my aunt (my mother's sister) who had accompanied me to the hospital was busy calling people telling them how I was in labor and was about to die. When I was at university and during my breaks, I would come down to her city and babysit her babies. I specifically remember staying awake all night with her last baby because this baby would be asleep all day and stay awake all night. No matter what they did, the baby would not stay awake during the day. To make things worse, this aunt of mine stole part of the money that I was to use to pay my hospital bill upon discharge. I discovered this when I was about to pay my bill. This left me even more devastated.

When I arrived home, and about one month later after resting, I decided to take a fast and asked God why He let this happen to me. I also asked God to reveal to me who had stolen the money. If it was a coworker in the hospital where I worked, I would be cautious with that person. To my greatest surprise, God told me my aunt stole the money and that I shouldn't worry. He was going to deal with her. I texted her the scripture which says, "If anyone returns evil for good, evil will not depart from his house" (Proverbs 17:13 ESV).

I thanked and blessed God for being my shield throughout this journey, for giving me victory, and for making my baby and me come home safely. God also told me that He wanted to use me to elevate the name of my OBGYN doctor since he was mistreated, misjudged, and accused wrongly by the hospital administration despite all his hard work in that hospital. The hospital administration despised him for wanting to quit following this treatment. The administration was hoping to use the failure of my delivery as evidence against him, especially if anything bad had happened to me or the baby. God says He used this opportunity to prove the administration wrong and prove this doctor was far more capable than they thought.

This aunt later was plagued with diseases and one series of calamities after the other. She is barely surviving as of this date. If you ever think that those you have stood for will stand by you when you need help, then you are in for the greatest surprise in your life. However, God has His way of repaying everyone for his or her wrongdoings or good deeds. Two friends of mine later told me that the day I was in labor, God woke them up at midnight and asked them to pray for me. They obeyed and prayed for me.

Two weeks after my baby and I were discharged, I was asleep and suddenly found myself returning home from somewhere. As I was returning, I saw a very tall man with wings carrying my baby. I stopped and asked him, "That's my baby. Why are you carrying him and where are you taking him?"

He responded, "Take your baby and run home. He was about to be carried away in that train over there." He then turned aside and pointed at a train that had many babies inside it. There stood a charcoal dark man with a long tail and two horns. He ushered babies into the train and the train was about to depart. I saw hundreds of babies sitting in the train and ready to be taken to some destination. The man then walked toward me and handed me the baby. He told me to run as fast as I could. I started running. As I was running, it started raining heavily. I used my clothes to cover my baby's face. As I ran, a huge German shepherd dog about my height started chasing me to get the baby. I ran faster but it came even closer. I stopped running and started praying. As I was praying, the same man who had handed me the baby appeared, and the dog ran off. Then the man told me to keep running and I continued.

As I ran and took a bend or corner leading to my home, a black leopard with fierce dark eyes suddenly appeared and started walking toward me. I stooped down, reached out for a handful of soil, and started throwing it at the leopard. As I threw the soil at it, I said, "I rebuke you in the name of Jesus." Each time I said these words, I threw the soil at it. It stood in one place and started staring at me while blocking my path so I could not proceed. Suddenly, about six to eight little angels with wings and dressed in white appeared between me and the leopard. They started dancing as they went around in a circle. With this, the leopard fled, and I ran off with my baby. I reached my apartment complex and opened a door downstairs and saw a man and a woman, fair in complexion, lying in bed. Then I remembered that my apartment was upstairs. I quickly shut the door and ran upstairs to my apartment. I went straight into my room and placed my baby on the bed. As soon as I placed my baby on the bed, I woke up from sleep. I looked at the time and it was exactly one o'clock in the morning.

When I realized what had just happened, I wept profusely. After that, I prayed and thanked God for this great deliverance and for saving my baby's life. I couldn't sleep for the next three hours. When I finally slept, Mary, the mother of Jesus, came and stood beside my bed. She asked me to go to church, buy a hand rosary, and place it on my son's hand. When I woke up, it was 6:30 a.m. I immediately rushed to the 7:00 a.m. Wednesday mass at the nearby Catholic church.

After mass, I bought this rosary and the priest blessed it. I took it home and placed it on my son's hand. My son wore this rosary on his hand for over one year. This incident did not stop playing in my head and I intensified my prayers and fasting. I prayed for the children I had seen being carried away and I prayed for the awakening of mothers and future mothers to be. I was fortunate that my baby had been saved because I always prayed for my baby even before I had him. These prayers went ahead of me and waited for the right time for me to see their results. If I had not been praying, my baby wouldn't have been saved. I want to assume that the babies I saw on the train came from prayerless mothers or mothers who had been prayerful but were weak at some point, allowing the devil to steal them. Every time I had the opportunity, I would talk to mothers about the need to pray for their children. I did my intercessions in private as well. As I prayed, the Lord showed me how these babies didn't necessarily need to be dead physically. They may have been alive, but their spirits had been taken away. However, they would grow up and turn out to be either autistic, have some kind of weird medical diagnoses, be thieves, or be those who will later cause outrageous things in society. My heart is heavy as I write these words. I cry out loud as I pray and plead with parents to wake up when it comes to praying and interceding for their children. No prayer is too small. It is never too late to start, even if you have never done it. Just do your part by praying and trust God to do the rest.

Later, I moved to the United States to join my husband. I got pregnant and was so sick during that pregnancy. Throughout that pregnancy, I felt like I was going to die. I could neither eat nor drink anything. About eleven weeks into this pregnancy during my clinic visit, the midwife told me she could not find the baby's heartbeat. The fetus was dead. I felt so devastated, and I cried to God. God told me if this baby were to be born, it wouldn't have been a normal baby. I stopped crying and praised God for delivering me from the burden of a lifetime. I offered God a thanksgiving offering: all of my savings. Two months later, I got pregnant again and I glorified God for His marvelous doings in my life. Five months into this pregnancy, a cousin of mine went to church with his mom. Another aunt, who had been gravely sick, was about to have major surgery. The pastor of the church told them they had a sister in the United States who was a warrior in Christ. They should inform me that God wanted me to pray for my aunt before she went for the surgery so she would not die in the process. When they told me about this, I obeyed by engaging in three days of prayer and fasting. To the glory of God, the surgery, though critical, was a success and my aunt recovered.

A month before the baby was about to be born, the baby flipped in my womb from anterior to breech position. This necessitated that a C-section be performed for a safe delivery. I was in denial, knowing that I did not have much help at home. I had a toddler, and my husband was going to school full time. I prayed and cried to God for Him to flip the baby around and even saw a specialist to help flip the baby. However, the specialist told me this was going to be a dangerous adventure as this could cost the baby's life and mine. Despite all my cries to God, He stayed silent and never sent a word concerning this matter. Then I knew it was His will for the surgery to be performed. Indeed, the surgery was a success. I ended up carrying my cute little princess. After I had this baby, a friend of mine who never knew I was pregnant called me. She said God asked her to pray for a safe delivery for me because I was about to have a baby. I blessed the name of the Lord, and I blessed God for my friend as well.

Three months later, when I was getting ready to start work, God sent me a helper who watched my kids as I went to work. When my baby was seven months old, I became pregnant again. Though happy, I was worried and anxious about how I was going to manage three babies. Again, God sent me another helper after the previous helper had left. I ended up having a baby boy. When this new baby was seven months old, I became pregnant again despite being on contraceptives. What was wrong with me and this seven-month mark? This time around, my husband and I were devastated. My husband was in school full time; I was in school part time and working full-time while managing all that was going on in our lives.

We were already overwhelmed managing three little babies, school, and work. Another baby was just going to be more work for us. I asked God why He made me get pregnant despite all that was happening in my life at the moment. I told God that even though I wanted a fourth child, this fourth one came too soon. Then four months into this pregnancy, the COVID-19 pandemic hit. Of those in the healthcare system, pregnant women were the first to be asked to stop working in order to protect the babies. That was how I stopped working and stayed home. I had adequate time to take care of my family and manage all that was going on in my life while being paid fully.

Meanwhile, the pandemic grew worse. News came that one of my coworkers had contracted this virus while caring for these patients at work and he died. Another was on a ventilator and life support. Hearing this, my husband and I begged God for forgiveness, for doubting His will and His plans for us. We blessed God for this pregnancy, after seeing that this pregnancy came to save us. I would have brought the virus home to my young babies or may have ended up like my coworkers. I cannot even imagine the worst of things that could have happened. We named the baby Jeremiah, which means "God is high," "God will uplift," or "God will loosen." Indeed, He is high because He sees the beginning of everything from its end. He cared about our safety more than we cared about the burden of an extra child.

Three days after having this baby, an angel of God came to me in a vision and told me that the devil was planning something evil against the baby. I should take the baby's clothes and insert each one into the Holy Bible. As he was about to leave, he asked me if I had heard the instruction and I answered, "Yes." He started heading out of my room through the window. Then, he turned back and told me to bring out all of the baby's clothes so we both could carry out this act together. I got out of bed, collected all of the baby's clothes from the cupboard, and placed them on the bed. Together with the angel, we slotted every single item of clothing into random Bible pages. The angel told me this was so when the devil shot his arrows at the baby, the Word of God embedded in the baby's clothes would act as a shield against harm. When I woke up that morning, I blessed God for His love toward me and my family. I also thanked the messenger, the angel, for coming to fulfill God's message to me and I read the Book of Jeremiah to my son each time I breastfed him.

About a week later, I took my son for circumcision, and it was botched. The doctor asked us to return a week later for a revision. Then, I remembered the vision I had with the angel. We returned as instructed and the revision was done. Unfortunately, there was an artery that wouldn't stop bleeding. The doctor cauterized it, and it stopped bleeding. We went home and I placed the baby in bed so I could get something to eat. Immediately, I returned. I decided to check the baby's diaper, and the baby was a pool of his own blood. I screamed as I called my husband. We immediately rushed the baby to the emergency room at the hospital where the baby was born. While my husband was driving, I had to apply pressure to the bleeding artery to reduce the pressure of the oozing blood. I was praying and speaking scriptures to the baby. As soon as we arrived at the hospital, the bleeding stopped. The doctors said they could not see the bleeding area and I had to show them the diaper soaked in blood. They did some blood draws and immediately requested an urgent transfer to the children's hospital. They offered to transport us in the ambulance, but I refused. We opted to drive the baby there ourselves in our car. I specifically wanted the baby in our car so that I could take control of the atmosphere and everything that was happening in my car through prayer and warfare. Besides, my car itself is one of my prayer war rooms.

We prayed all the way to the hospital. This was happening at night. We were welcomed at the emergency department, and they received the baby. They had received the results of the blood draws from the previous hospital and needed to do an emergency blood transfusion because the baby's hemoglobin was less than 5g/dL; the normal range is 14–24g/dL. When I placed the baby on the bed, with the light bright enough, I saw how my baby had become so pale, something I didn't notice in the car or at home or in the previous hospital. Five minutes after placing the baby in bed, the baby's eyes became fixed and his arms flaccid with no movement. I yelled and the nurse called a rapid response. Before I knew it, all the rapid response teams had gathered, and I began to pray warfare prayers again. They immediately transfused my baby and admitted us. Meanwhile, one of my prayer partners called me saying that God woke him up at 2:00 a.m. asking him to pray for my baby because it was not fine. He obeyed, prayed, and decided to call me in the morning to check on us. We also arrived at the children's hospital at 2:00 a.m. Glory to God! When we were discharged from the hospital, my husband and I offered a thanksgiving offering to God for saving our son's life and for all He had helped us overcome. This was a wonderful testimony as we saw God work in mysterious ways just to protect us. We will forever be grateful to Him.

We can attest to the fact that, throughout my pregnancy journeys, God always came through and delivered me from the attacks of the enemies aimed at me and my babies. As I prayed for pregnant women, so did God send people to pray for me whenever I had difficulties in my pregnancy journey. I have come to realize that when battles come your way when you are innocent, God will always protect and deliver you. All these served to fulfill God's word according to Psalms 34:19 (ESV): "Many are the afflictions of the righteous, but the Lord delivers him out of them all."

Glory be to God!

CHAPTER 6

THE JOURNEY TO FORGIVENESS

We attain freedom as we let go of whatever does not
reflect our magnificence. A bird cannot fly high or far
with a stone tied to its back. But release the impediment,
and we are free to soar to unprecedented heights.[8]
—Alan Cohen

What is one thing you grew up facing that you would never wish someone else to experience?

Allow me to go first. As I mentioned earlier, I spent half of the earlier part of my life living with my grandma. She happened to live with her eldest daughter, Sandra (real name withheld). Every now and then, it seemed that everyone feared I would end up like my mum. As a child who loved her mum, I would spend my time crying. Whenever I wanted to go back to my mum, I was always talked into staying so I could help my grandma. Coming from a polygamous family, my mother and her twin brother were the first fruits of my grandmother, the second wife to my grandfather. The first wife had just a daughter (Sonia) who was a lot older than my mother. When my grandfather died, my mother, her mother, and the rest of her six younger siblings relocated to the town where their

---

[8] "Alan Cohen Quotes," Quote Fancy, accessed November 5, 2024, https://quotefancy.com/alan-cohen-quotes.

oldest stepsister (Sonia) was living. One day, this sister woke my mom up at midnight and asked my mother to accompany her somewhere. My mom was about eleven years old at the time. As narrated by my mom, she said she was instructed to go to a graveyard, take off her underwear, and set it on a grave. Being respectful, she did as she was asked. After that, she took my mom home, leaving the underwear on that grave.

A couple of years later, my mom became pregnant and bore my older brother. After she had my brother, his father abandoned her. The chain continued. Each time she was intimate with a man, she became pregnant, and the man would abandon her. She had eight children with eight different men. She lost one along the way. Before she died, my mom learned this was because of a curse placed on her by the sorcerer at the graveyard using the underwear she left on the grave. The sorcerer wanted a young girl in exchange for this transaction. My mother happened to be the perfect fit. For Sonia's children to be protected, someone had to pay the price.

Back in the day, our grandparents never knew or believed in God. They believed in performing rituals from soothsayers, sorcerers, and herbalists. These myths were practiced in a typical African setting. Most often, the exchange of spirits takes place as evidenced by the way of life of the victim. With my mom, no matter how much advice she was given about how to avoid getting pregnant, it all fell on deaf ears. However, over time, as people began to know God, their mentality began to change. They began to abstain from practicing these rituals, at least to some extent. Years before dying, my aunt Sonia confessed, and she begged for forgiveness from my mom. The sad story is none of her children ended up getting the luck the sorcerer had promised.

Meanwhile, before marrying my grandpa, my grandma had two daughters from her previous marriage, one of whom was Sandra. How my grandpa treated my mum, and her twin brother made Sandra felt left out. Back in the day, twins were treated with so much love because of the cultural importance attached to having them. This was especially true because my mom and her twin brother were the first fruits of my grandma and grandpa. My mum's siblings struggled seeing this. Jealousy in families can often be caused by insecurities. People who feel inadequate, dependent, or insecure may be more likely to feel jealous. Jealousy can damage relationships and make it difficult to maintain relationships with said family members. Some might become malicious with their actions toward those of whom they are jealous. Sibling rivalry is a tale as old as time.

My mom challenged and passed a competitive examination to enable her to become a government teacher. She needed to pay some money to secure her spot. Her other siblings weren't the most supportive of this new venture. Upon hearing this, Sandra instructed the other siblings so no one would offer my mum the needed money. If any man wanted to marry my mom, Sandra would go see the man or his family and tell them not to marry or allow their son to marry. She said my mom was a horrible person and they would regret it later. Unfortunately for my mom, these men, together with their families, would back off. Sandra would entice these men so no one would tell my mom why they were backing off. Unfortunately for my mom, her father died when she was about sixteen years old. My grandma was left with eight children to raise all by herself. My mom kept relocating, hoping to find love or a better life in other cities. Each time she thought she had found love, the man would impregnate and abandon her.

As I grew up beside my mom, I saw her struggling to make ends meet for us. It wasn't easy. I would sometimes stay away from school so I could watch my younger siblings while my mom was at work because we could not afford a nanny. Whenever I had to go to school, my mom would take the younger ones to her teaching job and tell the principal that she had nowhere to keep the babies because she needed to work. It was one struggle after the other. When I moved to live with my grandma, things became even worse for my mom because I was of great help to her. However, by God's special grace, all my siblings grew up. Seeing my mom's situation, I would pray and fast for her for several years without results. I remember how I would dedicate an entire seven, nine, and twelve days of fasting and prayers just for my mom. I did this for almost a decade, but there were no signs of change from my mom. I decided to stop praying for her, thinking perhaps that was the will of God for her, or perhaps God would never answer my prayers because He seemed to be silent after all these years.

My grandma retailed and sold ripe bananas on a popular roadside. She had been doing this business and, when I came, it skyrocketed because I provided much help with it. We added fried and boiled peanuts and other famous street food. Business was going great and so was my education. I would always top my class. At the end of every school year, I would return home with a lot of books and other school gadgets that I would use the following academic year. I would even send some books to my younger siblings each academic year. The government also awarded me a scholarship every academic year for my excellent grades. I would give this money to my grandma. She would add to the business capital and buy more goods. When school started, the business would yield enough profit so I could pay my fees and buy the necessary textbooks. This continued for the next five years until my grandma traveled to the United States to help nurse her other grandchildren. My aunt Sandra relocated to a new neighborhood, and I moved with them because I was helping her with her house chores. I couldn't do this business again because I wasn't familiar with the new environment. Moreover, I was in high school, and my studies were becoming more intense.

When I lived with Sandra, she would always tell me horrible stories about my mom. Meanwhile, my grandma was in America, living with Sandra's daughter to help her with her kids. Sandra's daughter told my grandma that she had been sending money through her mom back to Cameroon to send me to school. My grandma was surprised at this and told her that she and I had been doing business and that was what supported me through school. This means that all along, Sandra had been collecting money from her daughter saying she was taking care of me. Meanwhile, she had never supported me through school despite me working for her and helping her with her house chores. Sandra had restrictions as to what she could do. She had gotten into a fight with her husband; he had beaten her and fractured her left arm. Upon attempting to repair the bone, the surgeon accidentally damaged nerves, which left the arm paralyzed. I would do all her house chores and cook and do laundry by hand since we didn't have washing machines. After that, I would still take care of my grandma and manage our business.

Personally, it was never a bother for Sandra not to give me anything because I had all my basic needs. However, to collect money from her daughter for her personal use and lie that she was the one sponsoring me shocked us all. Later, we even found out that Sandra had told some family members and friends that she was the one sponsoring me. This was absolutely heartbreaking. I remember how my grandma would get into fights with Sandra, asking her to assist with my education because I was doing a lot for her as well. Sandra would argue and it would turn into a huge fight between them. Once we relocated and I was living with Sandra with no business to do, things became extremely difficult for me. Feeling like you have no purpose and aren't appreciated can weigh heavily on your heart. I was devastated. I wept several times. On several occasions, I planned to escape, but a couple of friends advised me to finish high school since I was in my last year. They said if I left, it might be difficult to be accepted into another school since it was already the end of the school year. Relocating would have caused me to restart or possibly be a dropout. Adjusting to a new school or environment in my final year of high school could possibly affect my final examination results because I was already excelling in them.

Back then, phones were not common in my area, and I had no way of contacting my mom to explain all that was happening because she too had no phone. A few months later, my grandma returned from the United States very angry. She and Sandra's daughter didn't get along throughout her stay in the United States. By God's grace, I managed to finish my last year of high school and secured a job at a printing press. I was able to save some money from that job for my first year of university. When I left for the university, I knew that was it—I would never return to that house again. Completing university was quite a struggle, but I was able to do it and secured a job right after my final exams.

Meanwhile, my husband, who was our neighbor back in the day, had been seeing and noticing me. He came several times while I was in secondary school to date me, but I wasn't ready. I had a lot going on and dating was not on my list. About three years into working, he came again, proposing marriage. Then, he relocated to the United States. By that time, I was ready to get married as well. I prayed about it and the Lord told me that he was my husband.

As we were planning to get married, Sandra, who had been living in the United States, heard about it and decided to come back to Cameroon. She called me and said she was sorry for everything she had put me through and that she was ready to make things right. My mom and my grandma pleaded with me to let go and to let bygones be bygones. After all, she was family. I did not know that Sandra was looking for ways to get access to my husband and his family. Unfortunately, sometimes you have people in your life that only want to see you fail and it's a shame when you give them a second chance.

After the wedding, my husband moved back to the United States, and I went back to work in the city in which I was living. I gave birth and when my son was about seven months old, a friend of mine (the same one who had called me to tell me that I was going to have a baby the morning my water broke) called me. I had not been in contact with her for a long time and was surprised when I saw her call. She said an angel of God came to her, instructing her to call me and send me to a certain pastor to pray for me, and that I should be quick about it. She then sent me the pastor's cell phone number and I called him immediately. This was a Divine instruction, and delay was not an option here. The pastor was out of town and said he would get to me once he returned. A couple of days later, he called me and said he could come over to my place. Immediately he walked into my home and saw me. He said God had sent a message to save my marriage from any outside threats. He said God had specifically told all individuals questioning our marriage a message that this marriage was ordained by Him (God) and it would not be well with any person who tried to put it asunder. These individuals happened to be my in-laws influenced by Sandra. Meanwhile, Sandra had narrated my mom's life story to my in-laws and said that my mom and I were going to ruin their son's (my husband) life. The best thing they could do was to end the marriage. As I heard these words from the pastor, I froze. I would never have imagined that all this was happening. The pastor then prayed for me and my baby.

After the pastor left, I immediately called my husband. He was furious and immediately called all of his family. They all agreed to what the pastor had said. They told him they did this because they were trying to protect him. A bunch of horrendous things started happening to my husband's family because at first, they insisted that Sandra might be right. Seeing all these, they held a meeting and said this should be God fighting them. Then they decided to beg for forgiveness from me and my mom. It felt like I could never escape the heartache of my past. My husband and I wept.

We were devastated. How could people be this wicked? This was someone who had apologized and had promised to make things right.

Soon after my husband's family were convinced of all these lies, my own family started to disown me too. I knew I was under serious attack and so I intensified my prayers. I remember how the Lord instructed me not to associate with any of my family members and so I distanced myself from them. I did as instructed. Meanwhile, with all this happening, my mom had been diagnosed with leukemia when I was about five months pregnant. She had moved to live with one of her sisters because I was pregnant and needed help myself. My job was demanding and managing these two would have been stressful. Sandra called one of the daughters of this sister and asked her to insist they send my mom to me so that I could deal with her and my pregnancy. Hearing this, this daughter said they could never do such a thing because my mom was the one who took care of them while they were young. It was their turn to take care of her too.

That was the final straw for me. I exposed all that Sandra had ever told me about my mom and other family members, and she became even more enraged. About six weeks after I had my baby, my mom, though sick and fragile, insisted that she wanted to come over to see my baby. When she came, I was heartbroken. The full-fleshed, lively woman had become so pale from the trauma and emotional breakdown from this sudden diagnosis and dealing with all that her sister was doing to her and me. I had never seen my mom in this condition. It was devastating. I went into the restroom away from her sight and wept bitterly so she would not feel more depressed.

After I had calmed down, I dried my tears and stepped out to be with her. She lived with me afterward because I couldn't stand the thought of letting her go, especially after seeing her current situation. While living with me, we went from one attack to another. The more we prayed, the more attacks we received. I spent my entire maternity leave in prayer and fasting, begging God for her recovery. I couldn't even make any breastmilk for my baby, yet my boy was the healthiest and most handsome baby you could ever see. During visits to the clinic for vaccinations, the midwife always picked me out of the crowd of new mothers as an example of how to care for a baby. Little did they know that my baby was Holy Ghost-branded. He looked great not from breastmilk but from my prayer and fasting. The other babies had artificial milk as well. My baby's state of health and well-being was just the work of God.

One day, after an intense midnight prayer, we went to bed. One hour into my sleep, I saw that an insect had stung my left hand. I immediately jumped out of bed and my left hand was paralyzed. I couldn't feel it. I immediately engaged in warfare prayers, anointing myself and declaring restoration. About thirty minutes into the prayers, my hand was restored. My mom, hearing how I was praying, came out of her own room to find out what was happening. I explained my dream to her, and she began weeping. I told her not to weep since God had restored my hand. The following morning when I opened the door, I saw blood in front of my door. I prayed over it, anointed it, and cleaned it up, knowing God had given me victory.

When I went to bed that night, the Lord told me that because I had insulted Sandra, mocking her about her handicapped hand and promising to break the other hand, Sandra, in turn, had been planning to paralyze my left hand as well. That was the night she came spiritually to execute her plans. Because I prayed before going to bed, my prayers served as a weapon and wounded her on her way out of my house. I grew in stature in prayer.

One afternoon, my mom and I were taking a nap and we both had the same dream. In this dream, Sandra was on her way to see my boss at work. I had secured a well-paying job. She was planning to tell him and all the other sub-bosses all kinds of lies about me. She planned to entice them into believing her and firing me while I was on maternity leave. When my mom woke up, she came to my room and told me about this dream. We both had the same dream at the same time. My mom advised me to go ahead of Sandra to my boss and explain everything before Sandra could come. Early the next morning, I went to my assistant manager, who also happened to be a pastor. Being a man filled with God's spirit of discernment, he was able to immediately understand the spiritual atmosphere. He prayed for me and said he was waiting for Sandra, if she still insisted on coming.

About a week after this, the Lord instructed me to go back to this pastor (my boss) and ask him to pray for me for thirty minutes. I called him and said that was what God had instructed me. He asked me to come over and we started warfare prayers in his office. At the start of the prayer, I looked at the clock. When he finished praying, I looked at the clock again and thirty minutes had passed. His final amen came in at the thirtieth minute, even though he did not look at the clock. I was in awe! I saw the wonders of God. That night, I had a dream and saw how Sandra, seeing these prayers, turned her car and returned home. Our prayers had reversed her plans. I was constantly under attack but each time, God gave me victory.

With all this happening, my mom had to be admitted to the hospital a couple of times for blood transfusions following her diagnosis. It was time for me to go back to work after staying home for almost six months on maternity leave. My baby was three and a half months old. I went into prayers and cried out to the Lord, asking him, "God, how do I manage a baby, my sick mom, and a job and with no help?" My kid sisters had moved in to live with us, but they, too, were students. My mom was very sick, and every day was a new onset of another symptom to be managed. "The weight is too heavy on me," I cried. On the day I went back to work, my kid sister sent me words that my mom wasn't doing well. My brother sent words to one of my aunts who lived nearby to go check on my mom while I took permission from work. When my aunt got there, the situation was critical, and my mom needed to be taken to the hospital immediately. My supervisor told me she could only give me a couple of hours to see how things were. I had to return as soon as possible because they were short-staffed and had a lot of work.

When I arrived home, they had just placed my mom in a taxi to take her to the hospital. Seeing this, we agreed that they go ahead to the hospital while I finished work. I returned to work, and they took her to the hospital. I asked my mother-in-law to go be with my mom and I would join them later that evening. She agreed and immediately went to the hospital. I returned home from work. As I was getting ready to go see them at the hospital, I received a phone call that my mom had just passed away. "Oh no, oh no!," I cried. I was devastated; my siblings were devastated. We cried and cried, and my neighbors came to console me. I was inconsolable. I recall asking God why He let her die knowing that all those battles we had been through together were in vain. I wept and wept. Nevertheless, that was it; there was nothing anyone could do. My mom was dead.

About two days after her death, I had a dream that God came and took me up to the clouds. He made me enter a plane that was carrying several passengers including my mom. I saw my mom dressed in warm clothing with a shawl around her neck. She was staring at the window. I read her mind. She was wondering how the children she had left behind were going to cope in her absence. Her youngest child was just thirteen years old. God told me, *"I have answered all your past prayers about your mom. There she is on her way to Heaven. So go home and weep no more."* He immediately sent me back to earth and I woke up from my dream. I couldn't believe what had just happened. God Himself had taken me up in the clouds and spoken to me. He had given me a response Himself despite over a decade of prayers for my mom with no answer from Him. Yay! That lady who was termed a strumpet had made it to heaven. Yay! The prayers I had given up on were already answered but were just waiting for the appropriate time to manifest. Yay! God used me to win a soul to heaven. Yay! Many other people were making it to heaven because I saw a full plane. Both men and women were well-dressed and tucked comfortably into their seats. Just as earth is real, so is heaven. There is power in intercession. I danced and praised God for what He had done. I blessed His Holy name for counting me worthy of all these. From that day onward, I stopped crying as I prepared for my mom's funeral, knowing that my prayers had been answered. She was in a better place than on earth with all the things she had faced. The burial was a huge success, and my mom was laid to rest.

A year and a half passed after my husband submitted my documents and that of our son to the United States immigration services. We were waiting for an interview date at the American embassy in my country. Based on normal circumstances, waiting for an interview date should have taken a maximum of three to six months. I waited for eight additional months. My husband was tired of calling the immigration services asking them what was wrong. They kept saying there were no dates available, and they didn't know when one was going to be available. Knowing what I had been through already and knowing that this could be another attack, I engaged in prayers and fasting. I did this on several occasions, asking God why all this was happening to me. I lost a lot of weight, and my complexion darkened. My family members mocked me, saying that my husband had married me and abandoned me with my son. They said there was no way I was ever going to join him. I became discouraged.

One night, I dreamt about a friend of mine, whom the Lord had called into ministry. He said "Nicole, do not be discouraged. Come with me." He held my hand, and he climbed the rocky hill with so much speed, as if there were no obstacles in his way. He reached out to my hand and pulled me up. I became so encouraged and started climbing my own hill of obstacles with faith and courage. Hallelujah! When I woke up from that dream, my spirit was hyped, my downcast faith was elevated, and I began praying and praising God. I decided to give this friend of mine a call. He told me how the Lord had told him to start a ministry, and he was using his home on Sundays for prayer services.

The following Sunday, I decided to pay his ministry a visit. He lived in a different city, and I had to wake up early in order to arrive there in time. As I was pressing the outfit that I was going to wear, a large portion of the fabric burned. The pressing iron was not set to a high temperature, yet my outfit burned. I took another outfit, and the same thing happened. This wasn't normal. My sister said this must be the devil fighting my trip to this church. Indeed, this was a delay tactic. Then, I decided to wear an outfit that didn't need to be pressed. Thankfully, I arrived in time and the service was amazing. The sermon that day was about staying encouraged amidst adversities. I knew this was directed to me. After church service, I met with my friend one-on-one and shared with him all the difficulties I had been facing. We prayed. I returned home that evening.

When I woke up the next day, my husband called to tell me that I had been issued an interview date. I checked my email, and my interview was in two weeks. I couldn't believe this. This was the power of God at work again. I called my friend and gave him this exciting news. He told me that after I left that day, God instructed him to pray for me. Some people from my family had gathered and made declarations that my son and I would never join my husband. He spent hours that night praying for me. I was astonished. I remembered how God had instructed me to stay away from my family. I praised God even more.

Two weeks later, I went for the interview with my baby. When we arrived at the building, it began to rain heavily and there wasn't any shade as we stood outside. I used a blanket I had brought and covered my baby's face as we stood under a little shade. Suddenly, a man came running from nowhere and dropped a bag in front of where we were all standing. Then he ran away. The security guards instructed us to evacuate that area because there could be a bomb in the bag. Panic struck us and we all pulled away into the rain. One of the security guards approached the bag and turned it upside down as we all stood under the rain and watched. It turned out that it was the garbage of a mad man. They ushered us in, starting with those who had babies. Upon arriving in the waiting room, we were issued ticket numbers, and we were to be called for our interviews based on those numbers. As I sat in the waiting room partially soaked, I stared at the walls and their beautiful decorations. As I looked around, I heard my ticket number called. I approached the counter carrying my baby and was welcomed with a kind smile by my interviewer. My interview lasted about thirty minutes. I presented all the documents to prove that I was legally married to my husband and answered all the questions asked. At the end of the interview, the interviewer responded, *"Mrs. Bobga, there is no reason why I shouldn't give you this visa. Welcome to the United States of America."* I smiled in excitement, making sure to maintain a calm demeanor so people sitting around would not notice.

From the embassy, I boarded the next bus home and couldn't stop praising God on my way home. This scripture came to me: "Delight yourself in the Lord, and He will give you the desires of your heart" (Psalm 37:4 ESV). I kept praising God for His wonderful and marvelous deeds in my life.

My husband immediately paid for our flight, and we were to travel to join him in a month. This would give me time to resign from work and pack my bags. As I did all these, I kept thinking about telling my grandma, who now was living again with Sandra. I recalled all that she and I had been through and thought it wouldn't be fair to travel without telling her. Besides, I didn't know when I was going to return. Even if I knew, she might not be alive, and I did not want to live with that guilt. As I pondered whether to tell her or not, I remembered how the Lord had told me to stay away from my family. This was a very challenging thing to do because these were the people I knew growing up. To keep such great news from them left me in a dilemma.

A week before my departure, I told my closest neighbor about it and how I would love for him to check on my kid sisters in my absence. He was excited for me, and he begged me not to tell anyone, considering how wicked the world is. He advised me I could inform people once I was in the United States. I agreed, but deep in my heart, I said I was going to tell just my grandma and instruct her not to tell anyone. *How could I keep this news from my grandma, knowing how much she loved me?* I asked myself. The question was if she could keep it to herself, especially knowing whom she lived with. I pondered back and forth through these thoughts, thinking of what best to do. That same evening in our evening devotion, we used a devotional called *Our Daily Manna* by Dr. Chris Kwokpovewe, a Nigerian pastor. The devotional from that day talked about the story of a woman who had been selling one of Africa's famous street foods, puff puff and beans, for many years. Life was difficult for this lady, and she would cry daily, begging God to change her story. God finally answered her prayers and made her win the United States diversity lottery. After processing all her papers and getting her visa to travel to the United States, this woman decided to call her friends and family and organized a send forth party. The party was a success. Everyone ate, drank, and was satisfied. After the party ended, everyone left, and the lady and her children went to bed. A couple of hours later, thieves broke into the house and told this woman to give them her passport containing the visa. This woman pleaded with them not to take it and that she was ready to pay any amount of money they wanted. The thieves said they were not there for money, just the passport. They took the passport and went away. The person who sent the thieves immediately traveled to the United States using this visa. The woman called the immigration services, and they said there was nothing they could do. She went back and forth with them, but they couldn't trace that person. That was how this lady became frustrated and went back to the streets to sell her puff puff and beans.

At the end of the story, Pastor Chris wrote these words in bold letters: "*The Holy Ghost is saying to a user of today's devotional who has just had a visa and is about to announce it, this same thing might happen to you.*" I immediately dropped down to the floor and wept. Look at what I was about to do. Yet, God loved me so much that He kept this message for me on this very particular day. I wept and wept. After that, I thanked God for His magnificent nature. That was how I made up my mind not to tell my grandma no matter the circumstance. My husband, on the other hand, told his mother and a few of his sisters and warned them not to tell any of my family since they all lived in the same neighborhood. By this time, they had realized themselves and were solely on my side. Though I insisted they not be told, my husband said this was going to cause serious trouble between us and them. He was going to tell them but emphasize the need to keep it a secret. Because he insisted, I stopped arguing and went immediately to God. I sought His protection, knowing that the message about keeping my visa a secret had come from Him. He alone knew how He was going to protect me.

The day came for me to travel with my son. My son and I boarded our flight and left. Four hours into the air, I realized I had several incoming missed calls and messages. When we landed at our first stop in Morocco, waiting to be transferred into our connecting flight, I charged and turned on my phone. There were several missed calls and messages from my grandma. My heart leaped as I pondered who could have told her. At 5:00 a.m., she had called my kid sister, requesting to talk to me. My kid sister responded that I had gone to work, and she insisted that she wanted to talk to me. She kept calling throughout the day to see if I would respond but I didn't. When I arrived in the United States, and after resting for a couple of days, I decided to give her a call. She was furious, asking how I could travel without telling her. When I asked her who had told her that I had traveled, she said she had people around who told her. To this day, she has never told me how she found out about my trip. However, I thank God that she knew about my travel after I had left. At least my baby and I were protected. Glory be to God.

If there's one thing I have learned, it is to never send your child to live with someone who hates you. There is a high chance that this person will transfer this hatred to your child. That was the mistake my mum made. She knew all along that this sister had never liked her, yet she still sent me to live with her. My mum was naive, thinking family cannot harm you like an outsider can. She didn't know better. Some strangers are better than family. That is why sometimes, I love it when strangers help me because they don't do it out of any obligation. They just choose to be kind.

Each time I was under an attack, I would ask God why He would allow all these things to happen to me. Every time I asked this question, He would remind me of His word according to Psalm 34:19 (ESV), which says, "Many are the afflictions of the righteous: But the Lord delivereth him from them all." On several occasions, He directed me to His word in Isaiah 41:10 (GNBDC): "Do not be afraid—I am with you! I am your God—let nothing terrify you! I will make you strong and help you; I will protect you and save you." These words served to remind me that I was going through all this not because of a sin I had committed but because the Lord was using me to execute His plans while protecting me in the process. Then I realized that the more I was persecuted, the more God's protection encapsulated me. After each persecution, I realized that I would be favored in another aspect of my life or experience a major breakthrough. Each time I wanted to worry, I found a certain peace that I could not explain. The more I delved into God's Word, the more I found peace. There was always a word of encouragement there for me. The Lord will always tell me what next move to make, making me busy so I don't have the time to think or worry about all that has just happened or was happening in my life.

As time went by, I developed a thick skin to persecutions. I learned that each time I was betrayed or persecuted, I could go to God in prayer and offer it to Him. At the end of it, I realized that God would give me a peaceful heart. He did not necessarily punish those who hurt me or take away the situation, but He would give me peace amidst this situation. I could go about my business as if nothing ever happened. People around me would ask me why I was not worried about what had just happened. I would tell them that God took care of it, and, in exchange, He gave me peace. I had no better answer to offer.

While my in-laws have changed, and we are now best of friends, Sandra and some other family members have not. I have learned there is an extent of wickedness and betrayal you can forgive, but you should not give those people access to you again.

CHAPTER 7

YOUR MINDSET

Your mindset is a blueprint of your life.[9]
—Terri Savelle Foy

Your mindset determines how you show up in the world. Most often, this is in direct correlation to the amount of self-confidence you have. Self-confidence is a feeling of trust in one's abilities, qualities, and judgment. With self-confidence, you have an overall positive vibe about yourself and your abilities. Self-confidence gives you that personal, positive affirmation despite what others think or say about you. It plays a prominent role in your social interactions, personal development, and success in the various facets of life. When you have self-confidence, it does not mean you are proud. It means you trust your abilities so much that you don't let anyone talk you out of something. People with self-confidence most often have made worse mistakes, but the difference between them and those who do not have self-confidence is that the former do not dwell on their past mistakes. They accept the fact that they made mistakes, ask for forgiveness, and determine to move on, taking the lessons learned to the next phase of their lives. Studies have shown that people with self-confidence have a strong internal locus of control. According to psychologists, there are

---

[9] Foy, "Unlocking Your Dreams."

87

three powerful concepts that influence an individual's development of self-concept: self-efficacy, locus of control, and self-esteem.

Self-efficacy refers to an individual's belief in his or her own competence and efficiency. This is related to self-confidence because it focuses on one's perceived competence in a particular domain. Research has shown that simply believing in our own abilities actually improves performance. Let's take an example. Assume that you are preparing to take an examination on a subject that you find difficult. The fact that you believe the subject is difficult already creates a defeating barrier in your mind. The chances of effectively preparing for that exam will be slim and the chances of failing it will increase. On the contrary, you may believe this is a challenging subject and therefore you need to study hard in order to pass the exam. This already shifts your perspective and compels you to put in more effort to achieve this goal.

Permit me to share the story of a young girl in Cameroon. Cameroon was colonized by France and Britain. Out of the nation's ten regions, two regions speak English and eight regions speak French, making Cameroon a bilingual nation. To enforce this bilingualism, the system of education has made it a requirement that students in the English-speaking part of the country pass French in order to move to the next level. The same is true for the French-speaking part of the country. This becomes more rigorous as you move higher in academia. This girl, who was from the English part of the country, had a phobia for French. She managed to find her way through secondary school without learning French. At the university level, it was a subject students must validate before graduating.

On the day of the French exam, she sat in to the examination hall until about half-way into the exam. When the invigilator stepped out of the examination room, she twisted her examination paper, put it in the trash, signed on the attendance sheet that she submitted her paper, and left the examination room. The examiner returned and didn't notice her absence. At the end of the exams, he counted the students' sheets and found out that one student's examination sheet was missing even though it had been recorded as submitted. He reported this to the faculty, and they began investigating and interrogating this student. After mounting pressure on her, she then confessed what she did. She said she did this because she didn't know what to write and would have failed the examination anyway.

The disciplinary council then canceled all her courses for that academic year. It was a hard pill for her to swallow as she spent weeks sobbing and depressed. Finally, she retook the courses and scored a B in French. In addition to passing all the other courses, she was extremely happy for the grade she had in French. Now, let me ask you this: what do you think happened? The student in the first part of this story was different from who she became after the incident. This incident made her develop self-efficacy through self-confidence. What she had done put her in a spot that forced her to develop a belief in her own competence, which led her into passing French with B grade. Most often, circumstances in life force us to develop self-confidence depending on whether we choose to define the circumstances as difficult and quit or as challenging and develop methods to help us overcome them.

Locus of control refers to an individual's belief about the extent to which he or she has control over the outcomes of events in his or her life. Locus of control can be internal or external. Those with internal loci of control believe that they have a significant influence on the outcomes of the events in their lives through their own efforts, choices, and actions. They believe that their decisions and actions make a huge difference in events and that they have the potential to shape their own paths in life. They attribute their successes and failures to their hard work, intelligence, skills, and choices. Those with external loci of control believe that the events happening in their lives are as a result of external forces, like fate, luck, or other people.

Self-esteem refers to a person's overall sense of his or her value or worth. It is an important aspect of mental health and well-being, influencing thoughts, emotions, and behavior. With self-esteem, you develop confidence in yourself. You learn to appreciate, love and respect yourself despite your circumstances. Self-esteem silences your inner critic and uses the lessons learned from your past mistakes to work on improving your future. With self-esteem, you become insensitive to criticisms, or handle criticisms constructively and become resilient to the challenges that life throws at you. Self-esteem enables you to see your worth, even if those around you do not see it. Self-esteem puts a *stop* on self-doubt and enables you to live with an overcomer's abundance mentality. A few ways in which you can build your self-esteem are practicing positive self-talk, practicing self-care, not dwelling on mistakes of the past, deleting old useless mentalities, polishing old useful mentalities, learning new skills, building competence, setting realistic goals, and seeking support when needed, just to name a few.

Thoughts, mindsets, and reasoning all have energetic and magnetic properties that they emit from you to your environment. That is why our way of living attracts people of that nature. Our belief systems attract circumstances based on our beliefs. Dr. Cindy Trimm, in her book *Unstoppable*, asked, "Could things be the way they are because of the way you are?"[10] She asked this question several times in this book. I paused for a second to reflect on the meaning of this question as it applied to my life circumstances. When I examined my life, I noticed that over ninety percent of the good things I said would happen in my life ended up happening. For example, before getting married, I said that I would have four children and even made a four-tier cake to represent each child. God blessed me with four children. After my first bachelor's degree, I said I wanted to get married and have all my children before going back to school. That is what happened to me. When I moved to the United States, I decreed that within my fifth year of living there, I was going to buy my first house, and I did. I said that I wanted to work with Kaiser Permanente and with the United States government, and I am currently working in these two places.

These are just to show you the power of our thinking, our mindsets, and our words. Believing and declaring that you are already where you want to be, even if you are far from getting there, puts you in a momentum that stirs up things to shift in the direction of what you have declared. These mindsets, thoughts, and words have magnetic properties that attract those things in your direction. Just as we attract positive things, we also have the ability to attract negative things through our thoughts, mindsets, and words. In Job 3:35 (KJV), Job says, "The thing that I greatly feared is come upon me and that which I was afraid of is come unto me." Job's greatest fear attracted what happened to him. Fear has a powerful impact on our mindsets. When we fear something, we would not dare go near it or attempt it.

---

[10] Cindy Trimm, *Unstoppable: Compete with Your Best Self and Win* (Stockbridge, GA: Cindy Trimm, 2021), 29.

Changing your mindset often is not an easy process. It involves warfare as you try to let go of your old thoughts and replace them with new ones. This transformation does not come easily. However, a positive transformation leads to victory as you are empowered to see beyond your current view and do the impossible. Changing your mindset can enable you to make superior choices that will have life-changing destiny advancements.

Scripture tells us in Deuteronomy 30:19 (GNBDC), "I am now giving you the choice between life and death, between God's blessing and God's curse, and I call heaven and earth to witness the choice you make. Choose life."

Let's analyze the above scripture using the scenario below.

There was once a promiscuous lady who ended up having two girls, whom she didn't get to raise. These girls survived by being dependent on family members and friends for help. In the course of helping these girls, some family members and friends kept insulting them, saying they would end up like their mother. One of the girls married, had children, and built a beautiful home for herself and her family. The other lady gave up on life, made very bad choices, and ended up living just like her mother. Someone had the opportunity to bring these two girls together and interview them. The girl who had built a beautiful life said that every insult ever thrown at her made her work hard not to fulfil them. When they told her she would never be successful, she made sure she worked hard to be successful. When they told her she would be frivolous, she made sure she never dated a man and kept herself until she was ready for marriage. She said she made sure she chose the opposite direction of what they told her she would become and made sure she never ended up as her mother. Her sister, on the other hand, accepted everything they said she would become. She said to herself that she was better off becoming like her mother just like the people had said. The moral of this story is that what we hear affects what we know. What we know influences what we believe. What we believe impacts the choices we make.

I try to avoid statements like "life is unfair to me." If someone disappoints me, another person will always make it up to me. Life might be unfair because we expect love to come from certain people. Those people are just a few compared to the billions of people in the world and God can choose to use whoever he wants to bless you.

The Youth's Voice

> Do not let anyone look down on you because you are young but be an example for the believers in your speech, your conduct, your love, faith, and purity. (1 Timothy 4:12 GNBDC)

In Cameroon, our culture trains us to respect the elders and not talk back to them when they are talking. A child who talks back to his or her parents or elders is considered a disrespectful child or a badly brought-up child, as they will call it. When elders talk to a child, if the child keeps calm and does not talk back, then they will say the child is respectful. In the United States, I found the opposite here among youths. Youths here have their voices and are able to express themselves; their parents or elders listen to them. One day, I was watching a training video as a new hire for my new job. The video taught us to defend ourselves or respond, especially when a patient says something about us that's not true. The video referred to anyone who remained quiet in such situations as "guilty." Sometimes, when my supervisors at work said something to me, keeping quiet meant that I was being respectful even if I was not guilty. To them, it meant that I was guilty. In the United States in most circumstances, silence means guilt. In Africa, silence means respect.

While working as a nurse and being seven months pregnant, I had a supervisor who always picked on me. I had five patients, with one who was on restraints and another who was on chest tubes. The patient with the chest tubes was attempting to pull out his chest tubes. While I was struggling to take care of the patient on restraints, the other was able to detach himself from the chest tubes and almost fell out of bed. When I finished taking care of the chest tube patient, I went to see the restrained patient. Meanwhile, the supervisor walked in the room where I was and said I abandoned this patient. To make things worse, he called me in for a meeting and told the other supervisors how I neglected a patient to the point where the patient almost fell out of bed. With this, I blew up in anger. I stated I had noticed this particular supervisor always picked on me and that he could have helped the patient knowing that I was busy with the other patient. I told him how, on several occasions, I had been in the breakroom when other staff would complain and cry because of him. I used this opportunity to narrate all that he had been doing to me and the rest of the staff and how displeased we were with his management. You could see how surprised he was, and he ended up apologizing. This was bad timing for him because he had plans on running for the managerial position. After I told him these things, he dropped out of consideration for this position. He became more polite and helpful on the floor with the rest of the staff. The other supervisors in the meeting with me later thanked me and told me how proud they were of the things I told him and how I presented them. This made him take a 360-degree turn in his interaction with the rest of the staff. Whenever I was on duty, he would look for me and ask if I needed help. He later on resigned and went to work in another hospital. One thing I know for sure is that he will take the lessons he learned with him and be a better person wherever he goes.

Standing up for myself is something that I had to learn the hard way. Standing up for yourself teaches people how to treat you the way you want to be treated. I have learned that standing up for myself does not necessarily entail being rude. Instead, I will make my point in a way that will edify the other person or have a positive impact in his or her life.

Through reading 1 Timothy 4:12, I have come to understand that the younger generation is working hard to be the future while the older generation is fighting not to be the past. The younger generation responds to two things: love and respect. When we show love to the young, we minimize their weaknesses. Showing them, respect releases them into their strengths. Let's learn to empower the young people around us. Let's listen to them and give them the ability to express themselves. Let's learn to give them a voice. Let's not despise their youth. When change comes from the top, it is renewal, but when change comes from the bottom, it is revolution. We want a renewal and not a revolution because revolution brings fighting and chaos. When we give youths their voice, we affirm how important they are and make them feel respected. It also gives us an opportunity to learn from them. It can be so frustrating when you don't give a voice to your children, and you find them going to confide in someone else.

CHAPTER 8

CHOOSING FRIENDS

Your friend is a prophecy of your future, so choosing your
friends is as important as choosing your future.[11]
—Funke Felix-Adejumo

Friendship, whether with relatives or non-relatives, is an important
component in life. However, friends can either build you up or tear you
down. A good friend is a great asset while a bad friend is a liability. That is
why choosing the right friends is about finding people who enhance your
life. Choosing the right friends is about building meaningful and lasting
relationships. Investing time and effort into these relationships is pertinent.
Good friends are invaluable to your happiness, growth, and well-being. I
am sure you have heard the saying "you are who you hang out with." This is
true because you smell like the company you keep. Choosing your friends
is as important as the smell you want to carry around. Who we are, how
we act, how we think, and what we do starts with the friends we hang out
with. The company you keep has the ability to determine what your life
will look like in the future. Your friends are a prophecy of your future. How
your future will look is most often influenced by the people you mingle
with. Knowing this, we want to make sure that the friends we keep are of

---

[11] Felix-Adejumo Funke, Instagram, accessed November 5, 2024, https://www.
instagram.com/reel/C4_Mvf1rfdC/?igsh=MzRlODBiNWFlZA==.

quality not quantity. The big question is "how do you know that so and so person is or will make a good friend? Since we do not have a litmus paper to test who will make a good friend, we want to walk with wise company who are God-fearing. Such people seek to honor God in their daily dealings and will have a higher chance of loving us unequivocally. When it comes to forming friendships, personally, I only allow relationships that align with my life's dreams and goals. It does not have to be all my dreams but at least one or more of them.

Most often, we form close relationships with people with whom we have shared interests and values. These shared interests and values provide a strong foundation for mutual understanding. Some friendships are built after a serious conflict that has been successfully resolved. Personally, I take choosing friends as a very important aspect of my life. Friendship can be a medium through which you are either blessed or become a blessing. It can also be a medium for toxic decisions or bad life choices.

Take the example of Amnon, David's first son. Second Samuel 13 narrates how Amnon was a victim of a bad life choice (listening to the advice of his friend, Jonadab) that later on led to his death. While Jonadab was Amnon's cousin (son of David's brother Shimeah), the text refers to Jonadab as Amnon's friend. Amnon fell in love with his half-sister, Tamar. When he told Jonadab about it, the latter advised him to lay down and pretend that he was sick. He could request that his father send him Tamar to prepare him something to eat. Once he was alone with Tamar, he could use the opportunity to violate her. Amnon did exactly as Jonadab had advised him and ended up violating his half-sister, Tamar. This act caused Amnon's half-brother, Absalom, to kill him two years later. It's so funny how the Bible depicted Jonadab as a very crafty man. This shows that crafty people cannot make good friends because they are either out to set you up for failure or for their personal gain. In Amnon's case, Jonadab was setting Amnon up for failure and, consequently, death. On the other hand, if Jonadab had advised Amnon not to nurture such feelings but kill them, this story would have been different. Moreover, she was not his wife. I believe that if we take this route of the story (the route where Jonadab had advised Amnon not to nurture such feelings), Amnon would not have made the decision that cost him his life. Compare this story to that of David and Jonathan, Saul's son. The great counsel of Jonathan to David caused David to escape death on several occasions. In the same way, our friends or family members can lead us to make the right decisions that will uplift or save us or the wrong decisions that will destroy us. That is why choosing friends is as important as choosing a spouse. The choice of friends has now become a spiritual thing. Praying for whom to consider or take as friends is as important as choosing your spouse. I believe that there are pertinent considerations to make before calling someone a friend.

The Book of Proverbs in the Bible provides some guidance when it comes to choosing friends. A typical example is Proverbs 22:2425 (GNBDC): "Don't make friends with people who have hot, violent tempers. You might learn their habits and not be able to change." In addition, Proverbs 28:7 (GNBDC) says, "A young man who obeys the law is intelligent. One who makes friends with good-for-nothings is a disgrace to his father."

Maintaining Friends

After choosing your friend(s), what next? When you finally find good friends whose spirits agree with yours, it is very important to keep them. Proverbs 18:24 (GNBDC) says, "Some friendships do not last, but some friends are more loyal than brothers."

In his book *The Seven Resolutions*, Karl Clauson shares an important technique on how to keep close those we call friends. He uses the acronym CARE.

C means to challenge your friends to grow spiritually. Encourage them to engage in activities that are geared toward Christ. Engage in activities and conversations toward matters of faith.

A means affirming your friend's value. Tell your friend how important he or she is to you or how much you appreciate something that person once did to you. Express how grateful you are to God for him or her. You can do this with a surprise gift, flowers, a note, or a text with kind words, a surprise visit, or whatever you think will make your friend feel valuable, appreciated, and loved.

R means respecting the wishes and feelings of those around you. If a friend tells you he or she does not like to be called, treated, or talked to in a certain way, please respect the person's feelings. That way, your friend will feel valued, and this will keep your relationship growing.

E stands for encouragement. Encourage your friends through compliments, by supporting them in their moments of weakness, or helping when they are going through rough situations. This can be done either through prayers, paying them regular visits, or through emotional, spiritual, or financial support. Practice encouraging them so they feel better or more comfortable when around you or after being with you. Let them go home and be able to laugh about a joke you made, fondly remember your conversations, or recall how you articulated yourself in a way that created a lasting happy impact on them. Try to make the small time you spend with your friends memorable. After your encounter with your friends, let them want to meet with you again. Never forget to apologize whenever you notice that you crossed their boundaries and make things right the next time. No one is above mistakes. What distinguishes a mistaken mistake from an intended mistake is a sincere apology followed by a change of character. Always remember that a good friend is a great asset, and a bad friend is a great liability. A good friend will make you gain something that you will be grateful for all your life. A bad friend will make you lose something that you will regret all your life. Choosing your friends is as important as choosing your spouse, as mentioned earlier. Just as we are being taught to pray for God to show us if the suitors who come our way are our destiny spouses, I think it is equally important to pray to God to show us who real friends are, even if the friendship may not last for a lifetime.

Let's again take the example of the friendship between Jonathan and David. First Samuel tells us that when they saw each other, their souls/spirits joined with each other. Jonathan went against his father's wishes just to protect his friend David. Some people have an approach to forming friendships different from that of David and Jonathan. Maybe you are the type who prefers to call someone a friend after years of testing his or her loyalty. Maybe you do not like making friends because of past betrayals or other reasons. Maybe you form better friendships and relationships with your blood relatives rather than non-blood relatives. Always remember that friendship is an important component of one's life, be it with your family or non-family. Proverbs 27:17 (GNBDC) says, "People learn from one another, just as iron sharpens iron." We all need friends from whom we can learn. True friends accept corrections, learn from them, and change their ways. Fake friends deny their faults, give flimsy excuses for their actions, and don't change their ways despite your advice and cautions. Rather than saying sorry, fake friends gossip and spread lies about you.

Over the years, I have come to realize that there are five main different ways that people tend to react after hurting you.

The first set of people will tell you they are sorry and really mean it, as evidenced by their positive change of ways toward you. Often, this even builds a stronger bond between you two in the long run.

The second set of people do not openly apologize but their facial expressions, body language, actions, and interactions when you are around them say it all.

The third set of people say they are sorry but try to justify their actions and blame something you did for making them react the way they did.

The fourth set are people who will tell you they are sorry but do not really mean it. They are just looking for ways to get closer to you and hurt you more. This happens especially when they know that you will forgive them and let them back in.

The fifth set of people are those who do not say they are sorry after an act. They spread lies to others about you.

In one way or the other, we all have encountered at least one of these situations. However, how they react will determine our next course of action and interaction with them.

Personally, I firmly believe that it is a privilege for someone or a friend to visit you or attend your party or event. It is not obligatory for someone to attend your event. As the organizer, you want to create a lasting positive impression and encourage the person to want to attend your subsequent events. In the events that I have attended, I have noticed that some people will use events to humiliate other people. For example, if a friend has a grudge against another friend or person, that person will wait for an event to bring it up, thereby sparking a fight. The person wants to use this opportunity to humiliate the other person by exposing the other person's secrets, faults, or acts to all those present, thereby create a lasting negative impression of this person to others. First, this is a humiliating act and, second, you are ruining the organizer's party. This unnecessary drama could have been avoided by the two people having a mature conversation with each other. Sadly, these days, there is hardly a party held with no incident of people quarreling or fighting. My question to these people who stir up fights is this. Have you ever considered that after this incident at the party, people will forever remember the party as one in which this and that person quarreled or had a fight? Is this how you want to be remembered whenever people recall an event? Think about it. As you think about it, allow this scripture to sink in: "Stupid people express their anger openly, but sensible people are patient and hold it back" (Proverbs 29:11 GNBDC).

When someone attacks you in public, I know it is only human to want to defend yourself. However, consider saying something like "Can we talk about it after this party?" Then, walk away from the person or the party. This shows great maturity and respect both for yourself and for the party organizer. I have experienced situations where people attack someone in public and then return to apologize for their acts in private. My question to them is: "Why not go back to that public place and apologize?" To me, this is character assassination where the person deliberately destroys another's reputation and character. These people expect to be forgiven right away when they ask for forgiveness. Often, their request for forgiveness may not be genuine. Forgiving these kinds of people should be a process. As you work toward forgiving them, educate them how to treat you by setting boundaries. Remember that these boundaries are not to keep them away, unless that is necessary, but to keep you together. Draw your necessary boundaries and stay consistent with them. You draw necessary boundaries with such people for the sake of your sanity. Boundary setting is for your own growth and health. Though this forgiveness is a process, it will need to be done because it releases our need for retaliation. Retaliation exposes us to Satan's accusation and God's judgment, as mentioned in Chapter 1. Your future is too full of unlimited possibilities to allow unforgiveness to blur it.

Personally, I stopped arguing with people, especially in public, because God didn't call me to win arguments but to win souls. Moreover, I am a witness of God and not a lawyer. I believe that you can say what you mean and mean what you say without saying it in a mean way.

The Book of Job 36:13 (ESV) says, "Godless people cherish anger." If you engage in a fight in response to the other person, you have behaved godlessly. However, there is what we call "righteous anger." This is when you are angry at sin and oppression. It happens when you have many reasons to be angry at something that is not right. However, unrighteous anger occurs when you become angry from something out of your own selfish desires. Still, all these are your decisions to make. Instead of carrying out unrighteous anger, you can choose to apply Psalm 26:11 (ESV), which says, "But as for me, I shall walk in my integrity; redeem me and be gracious to me." Walking in integrity is a choice. Your life is louder than your speech. As a child of God, whenever you compromise, know that people are watching.

CHAPTER 9

WILDERNESS EXPERIENCE

The wilderness is a place of preparation and not permanence.[12]
—Lisa Appelo

Each one of us has been betrayed by the very ones we love, to the point where we do not want to mingle with them and tend to isolate ourselves. After suffering so much betrayal from both families and friends, I have learned that most often, betrayal happens when you put your trust and confidence in a person rather than in God. When you trust a person more than God, He makes sure that He causes that person to betray you so you can run back to Him. Yes, God can be that jealous! After you come back to Him, you will feel a deeper connection with Him. Most often, God allows us to be betrayed by our loved ones and friends so that we have wilderness experiences. The wilderness experience occurs when we seek to isolate ourselves from the norms around us in order to find solitude, reflect on experiences, and gain a deeper appreciation of life without the norms. Spiritually speaking, the wilderness experience is where God takes everything from you so you can be empty and trust only Him. Unfortunately, our redeemed status as children of God does not

[12] Lisa Appelo, "The wilderness is a place of preparation and not permanence," Lisa Appelo, accessed November 5, 2024, https://lisaappelo. com/3-truths-when-youre-in-the-wilderness/wilderness-a-place-of-preparation-not/.

automatically prevent us from making bad choices. We live in imperfect bodies in an imperfect world, and such choices can lead us into wilderness experiences. Wilderness experiences can also be self-inflicted, like when you are having your moment or during a personal spiritual fast. These experiences can be very transformative, creating lasting memories and renewed perspectives in life. They serve as means of personal and spiritual growth where you find a profound sense of peace and connection with God. You will be amazed at how much insight you can gain from a wilderness experience. You will learn to rely on God alone and to be self-sufficient.

Before God takes you to the next level, He separates you. This is not loneliness because you are with God. He separates you from others because He wants to give you the tools necessary for your destiny. Another reason why He separates you is because He wants you to know His voice clearly. He wants you to be able to recognize His voice when He speaks to you, so you don't mistake Satan's voice for His. Often, when we are surrounded by so many voices, we can't hear God's voice. He will isolate you and put you through tests to train you to know and be able to recognize His voice amidst other voices. Another reason why God separates us is to make us unrecognizable to the people who knew us based on our backgrounds, past lives, and past mistakes. Train yourself to get used to isolation in God because that's the best time for gaining virtues that will help you distinguish God's voice from the others. When God removes people from your life, just know that seasons have changed. That is why some relationships will never be mended. When God removes people from your life, especially those who have hurt you and caused you to end the relationship, do yourself a favor and don't end the people. By ending the people, I mean don't try to take away the source of their livelihoods. If you do this, you will become a bad person yourself and you are no different from them. Sometimes, God allows bad things to happen to us because He wants to prune us to fruition. The size of your calling is equal to the size of your persecution. Most often, persecution causes you to experience the wilderness as you begin to question if God truly exists or if you are trusting the wrong God.

Wilderness experiences are either going to kill you or make you stronger. The wilderness builds you up. It builds endurance, compassion, patience, meekness, wisdom, insight, and other pertinent values and virtues. We all have had moments of wilderness experiences. They could be your marriage, your teen child, that addicted family member, your autistic child, your family's past, your parents, and so on. Most often, we do not choose the kinds of wildernesses that we will go through. Life forces them on us, or God chooses them for us.

Often in our wilderness experiences, God will kill some aspects in our lives that were serving as barriers for a genuine relationship with Him or with others. God uses these experiences to prune unwanted habits and experiences that are difficult for us to let go. These experiences affect our current ways of life. He then uses the wilderness experience to wither these past experiences.

How we overcome or succeed in these wildernesses depends on how we allow fear to overtake us. During these experiences, God will not talk to you like He is talking to person. He will talk to you like He is talking to Himself. That is why whatever He promises may seem impossible to us, especially given our current circumstances. However, He is talking to us based on the future He has for us. Through the training received from our wilderness experiences, God can give us potential that will cause us to move from obscurity to fame. A typical example is King David killing Goliath. While caring for his sheep, David was alone with these sheep; he was their shepherd. When any bear or lion came to attack his sheep, he would kill it with his bare hands. This occurred once or twice until David mastered the art of killing the attackers (lions and bears). That is why he was able to go boldly to Samuel and tell him he was able to kill Goliath. No one believed him, not even Saul and Goliath (see 1 Samuel 17:43). David was convinced that the training he received when no one was watching would be his source of victory (see 1 Samuel 17:36). That is why it is ungodly to stop someone with positive creative ideas from expressing or attempting them. The training and skills that David received and learned during his wilderness experience coupled with the God he believed in enabled him to defeat Goliath. The training and victorious revelatory mindset that David had gave him the supernatural victory of killing mighty Goliath. Some texts say that Goliath was around nine feet nine inches tall while David was shorter than five feet. Wow David! If David just had faith in God without the training he received in the wilderness, he wouldn't have defeated Goliath. Similarly, if he had the experience without God, he wouldn't have defeated Goliath. Therefore, the training we receive from the wilderness experience work hand-in-gloves with our faith in the One who put us through these experiences.

The take-home message here is that your mindset and thoughts have to be backed up by action and a belief system. Who and what are you believing in to help conquer that Goliath in your life? When you want to achieve something, what steps do you take toward achieving it? Who do you believe will help you achieve it? I'll let you ponder on these questions.

Victory, success, poverty, wealth, good health, abundance, defeat, and so on all require mindsets to be expressed in. Blessings and curses both require a mindset to be expressed in. Your mindset has the ability to deflate or inflate your potential for success. Your mindset has the ability to shape your destiny for good or for worse. Scripture tells us in Isaiah 8:20 (KJV), "To the law and to the testimony: if they speak not according to this word, it is because there is no light in them." The amount of spiritual illumination you have on the inside has a great role to play in your mindset. The amount of light in you determines the things that come out of your mouth about your destiny. The affirmations you make about your life determine the course of your life. The things that come to you are those that find a component within you that draws them to you. It is not enough to declare things; you must also believe them to be possible for you. Both of these (declaring and believing) attract the success of whatever you believe in.

I bet you will be surprised if I told you that God is a businessman. He is a transactional God. He will take you to this wilderness in order to exchange your flaws and past mistakes for something that will be used by other people who are going through similar situations. He exchanges "this" for "that." That is why the wilderness puts you into a place of being corrected. When in the wilderness, by default, our natural inclination is to say, "God, please get me out of this" or "God, why me?" However, when we ask the question, "God, what are you teaching me?" we invite God to teach us aspects we have never seen before. As someone who has been in the wilderness on several occasions, I know that after my wilderness experiences, I become more blessed. I am tempted to call my wilderness experiences my *"wilderblessed"* experiences. It does not matter if the change has to take place in me or in the people around me; I am still blessed. My wilderness experiences are my moments of favor where God shows me tough love. No matter how tough God is during our wilderness experiences, let's always remember that God is for us. His purposes for us are to prosper us and to draw us closer to Him than we were before. During our wilderness experiences, God shows His transactional nature or character. He removes "this" in exchange for "that." He takes our anger and lack of patience and replaces them with trials that will enable us to gain perseverance and meekness. He takes out doubt and replaces it with faith. He takes out ignorance and replaces it with abundant knowledge. He takes out cowardice and replaces it with bravery. He takes out fear and replaces it with confidence. He takes out doubt and replaces it with faith. The list goes on. How we come out of the wilderness determines our eligibility for God's promises to be fulfilled through us or not. If we come out refusing to change, God is able to skip us and decide to use the next generation or someone else instead to accomplish His will. However, if we come out pruned and transformed, God will elevate us beyond measure.

Many times, while in my wilderness, I have told God I want to give up and that I can't continue. A typical example is the writing of this book. Most often, I heard God telling me the next person He is going to use if I do not want to take the mantle. Then I remember the story of Esther in the Bible (please reference the Book of Esther). It is important to note that your wilderness is not a place of pampering but a place of tough love. It is a place to gather your courage and prove your faith even if you do not have enough. God in His infinite mercy will help you overcome. I learned to pray for grace to victoriously overcome my wilderness experiences rather than ask God to take them away. I learned to pray audacious prayers. I learned to fight differently and make bold decisions as long as they are in line with God's will. When we use our wildernesses to whine, God has the ability to stretch or extend them. Your response to your wilderness determines how long your wilderness will last. The more you keep complaining, the more the wilderness will be extended. However, the more you call on God, the more He will come to your rescue and give you strength despite your struggles. He will give you tiny bits of victories and strength even within those wilderness experiences, without you even noticing them sometimes. Often during these wildernesses, God is so silent that you will be tempted to doubt His existence. It is important to know that God is working behind the scenes even if it does not seem like He is. That is why we feel that He is silent. This is the moment when we should be still and know that He is God according to Psalm 46:10. It's a period where our emotions die so that our faith can grow.

Whenever you find yourself in your wilderness experience, remember the story of Job in the Bible. When Job's wife came and asked him to curse God and die, Job asked her, "Shall we receive good from God, and shall we not receive evil?" (Job 2:10 ESV). Just as God did it for Job, He will do it for us, too. I firmly believe in Romans 8:28 (ESV), which says, "And we know that for those who love God all things work together for good, for those who are called according to his purpose." I believe that in the end, God will work all things out for our good and for the good of generations to come. The only way to survive the wilderness is through the Word of God, through our faith in the Word of God, and through worship. Weapons of victory are released when we worship in our moments of wilderness. We survive by every word that comes out of God's mouth. The wilderness is a place of wanting. However, we should never let our wanting turn to weariness. Weariness turns to whining and whining turns to wickedness. Rather, let our wanting turn to waiting, waiting turn into worship, and worship turn into winning.

CHAPTER 10

AUTHENTIC LIVING

The most exhausting thing you can do is to be inauthentic.[13]
—Anne Morrow Lindbergh

If I asked you, "Who are you?" what would be your response?

Would you answer me with your profession, occupation, or your current status in life? Would you answer me with what society has labeled you? Would you answer with what people have been telling you about yourself? Sadly, many people do not know who they are. You will hear people say, "I am trying to find myself," or "This profession is not for me," or "I chose the wrong college degree."

Let me rephrase my question and ask you, "Who does God say you are?" I will leave you to ponder your answer to this question. If you have found your answers to this question, then ride on with me.

The challenge to living authentically provides guidance to answering this question. The big question is what is authentic living?

Authentic living involves being true to oneself, embracing one's values, beliefs, and desires, and acting in ways that align with one's true nature. It is a call to everyone, no matter their race, religion, or location. It refers

---

[13] Anne Morrow Lindbergh, "The most exhausting thing you can do is to be inauthentic," The Quotations Page, accessed November 5, 2024, http://www.quotationspage.com/quote/25698.html.

to living a life that reflects who you genuinely are rather than conforming to external, societal norms. Manifesting your true self requires that you live authentically. Authentic living means living beyond your role or title. Authentic living is not the absence of sins, faults, or bad choices but the ability to recognize our faults and apologize for them. Unfortunately, our redeemed status as children of God does not automatically prevent us from making bad choices because we all live in imperfect bodies in a fallen world. However, not dwelling on our imperfections and letting them define us but using these imperfections to edify ourselves helps shape our paths to authenticity. Authentic living prohibits you from defining yourself by your past mistakes or by the mistakes of your ancestors. Authentic living allows us to live the best possible versions of ourselves. This, in turn, places us in competition with no one else but ourselves. Authentic living exposes us to preeminence.

Authentic living compels you to live a Christ-like life, a life that our Heavenly Father would be proud of. This is because our God is an immutable God, meaning He does not change, as stated in Malachi 3:6. His true nature is *authenticity*. Who we are and the way we live counts before God. God is looking for those who present themselves honestly before Him. Your authentic divine self is the seed of greatness that God has placed inside of you. How and with what you nurture this seed will determine the kind of fruits you produce and how you live. The Book of Colossians 1:27 (ESV) says, "Christ [is] in you, the hope of glory." This means that when God created us, He placed Christ as seeds in our hearts. With Christ in our hearts, we hope we will let Christ refine us so we can live in glory and authenticity. Living authentically requires us to prune unwanted habits and cultivate and nurture authentic habits. It requires some trimming, resizing, abstaining, deleting, adding, planting, and nurturing some habits. It requires us to cut any ties that will keep us emotionally connected to old methodologies, cycles, patterns, seasons, and limitations. It also requires us to learn new skills, create new relationships, and dare to accept new opportunities that will help propel us to where we are heading or to living the life that God has called us to live.

Steve Maraboli, a life-changing speaker, bestselling author, and behavioral science academic said, "Live authentically. Why would you compromise something that is beautiful to create something that is fake?"[14] This question hits home. We were given the chance to live so we can achieve our optimum selves, to live unapologetically purposeful lives, and to do so fearlessly. Authentic living has valid proof to back it up. This proof is *excellence*. Authentic living exposes you to excellence. Excellence involves going beyond what you will normally do. It involves outperforming your last performance. Outperforming your last performance exposes you to excellence in character, in raising godly children, in academics, and in your career, just to name a few. Authentic living and excellence are both contagious. This means that you are able to change the trajectory of another's life for good by your authentic lifestyle.

In secondary school days, I would earn good grades in my subjects because I paid attention to every detail given by my teachers during class. I would work extra hard to earn excellent grades. At the end of each examination, I saved my test papers. Years later when I was in university, I visited an aunt in a nearby city. That city was known to have the highest number of school dropouts. The girls would mostly leave after the second or third year of secondary school, mostly because of pregnancy. These girls most often ended up roaming around the city living frivolous lives. Between the ages of fifteen to twenty, most of these girls were already mothers with absent fathers. There was a particular girl who was about my age (nineteen years old then) who already had a five-year old daughter. She left school in her third year of secondary school because she became pregnant. She often came to visit my aunt and that was how I got to know her. In one of my conversations with her, I asked her if she had plans of going back to school. She responded that it was over five years since she left school. She did not know if she could ever comprehend the material if she had to go back to school. I then encouraged her that it was possible for her to start all over despite being away from school for this long. Whenever I visited, I kept encouraging her and she promised to give it a thought. I brought her my past test papers for the class she had promised to start. I told her to keep them and use them whenever she was in school. I also promised more test papers for her as she advanced. She took them and kept them.

Years later, after I had graduated from the university and had started

---

[14] "Steve Maraboli Quotes," Goodreads, accessed November 5, 2024, https://www.goodreads.com/author/quotes/4491185.Steve_Maraboli.

working, my phone rang one day. This girl called to tell me that she had completed high school and had been admitted into a professional school to become a secondary school instructor. I was flabbergasted and requested that she pay me a visit. When she visited, she told me how she woke up every morning and reviewed those tests and exam papers that I had given her while asking herself what I did to get all those high scores. She told me how she would ask herself if she too could achieve such high scores. She said she bought the newspapers containing my secondary and high school national exit examination results and she would see that I topped my school. She said she reviewed those test questions and answers so much that she memorized them and knew them by heart. One year after having these papers, she decided to enroll in school. She said if I could get these results, she could, too. At every class level, she strove for the best scores, just like I had on those papers. Although she did not ace all the subjects, she never failed a test. She kept going forward. When she received admission into this professional school, she said the first person who came to her mind was me. She said wanted to thank me for being such an inspiration to her. I was touched seeing how the excellence of my past had been such an inspiration to another lady. I blessed God so dearly for her.

Do you see why I say authentic living is contagious? Do you see why I say authentic living and excellence work hand-in-glove? When you live authentically, do not think or assume that you are doing it for yourself. You might be the Bible that others are reading. You might be the hidden or secret coach for others. When you live a fake life, you are encouraging people around you to live fake lives as well. However, when you live an authentic life, you are like a city built on a hilltop whose light shines bright for others to see and be motivated. Why do you want to compromise something as beautiful as living authentically?

Authentic living sometimes involves taking risks and risks puts you into the realm of faith, so your faith is stretched beyond your imagination. Living authentically does not mean that you need to live a perfect life. It is important to note that excellence is different from perfectionism. Let's take a moment to explain the difference between excellence and perfectionism. Perfectionism is the belief that if you can do something perfectly, people will love and accept you. If they don't, it means you are not good enough. Perfectionism leads to inferiority, low self-esteem, and isolation. Below are a few definitions that will enable you to differentiate between excellence and perfectionism.

Excellence is a mindset while perfectionism is an activity.

Excellence is an act of being while perfectionism is an act of doing.

Excellence is to be in order to do while perfectionism is to do in order to be.

Excellence is indispensable while perfectionism replaceable.

Excellence is about adding value while perfectionism is about gaining attention.

Excellence is character-driven while perfectionism ego-driven.

Excellence is grand-conscious while perfectionism is self-conscious.

Excellence is cooperation while perfectionism is competition.

Excellence is risk-oriented while perfectionism plays it safe.

Excellence is about the process of achieving a goal while perfectionism is about getting it done.

Excellence is success-minded while perfectionism is failure avoidance.

Excellence involves seeing failure as a growth tool while perfectionism involves seeing failure as a disaster.

Excellence is pleasure in pursuing purpose while perfectionism is anger and frustration in pursuing purpose.

Excellence involves life lessons while perfectionism involves no lessons.

Excellence is led by vision while perfectionism is driven by vision.

Excellence is being open to the new while perfectionism is close-minded.

Authentic living produces excellence. Excellence goes beyond just the "good enough." It makes you shine in your domain. Excellence makes you a person of value and increases your value, adding equity to your relationships or business. Your value determines who and what pursues you. You will automatically become an influencer, and success will automatically follow you. Living authentically and excellently is a mindset. As you put your mind to them, they allow you to be outstanding, to be second to none, and to surpass expectations. When you make authentic living and excellence a lifestyle, you will outdo, outperform, outstand, and outclass the people in your circle, age group, and beyond. They will compete with you, but you will never compete with them because you will be the best, the GOAT (greatest of all time) and head and shoulders above all.

Therefore, as we all strive to live authentically, let's remember this.

Don't just exist; live.
Don't just live; attempt.
Don't just attempt; explore.
Don't just explore; read.
Don't just read; absorb.
Don't just absorb; learn.
Don't just learn; think.
Don't just think; communicate.
Don't just communicate; hear.
Don't just hear; listen.
Don't just listen; understand.
Don't just understand; contribute.
Don't just contribute; act.
Don't just act; teach.
Don't just teach; prove.
Don't just prove; experience.
Don't just experience; change.
Don't just change; evolve.
Don't just evolve; transform.
Don't just transform; promote.
Don't just promote; promise.
Don't just promise; demonstrate.
Don't just demonstrate; relate.
Don't just relate; advocate.
Don't just advocate; reinvent.
Don't just reinvent; influence.
Don't just influence; encourage.
Don't just encourage; see.
Don't just see; feel.
Don't just feel; dream.
Don't just dream; do.
Don't just do; *excel*.

CONCLUSION

Honestly, writing this book has been one of the instructions I have had to reluctantly obey. I was full of doubts and felt discouraged several times along the way. I felt weakest whenever I sat to write this book. However, God's Word, according to 2 Corinthians 12:9 (ESV), is, "My grace is sufficient for you, for my power is made perfect in weakness." This verse came through for me and gave me strength beyond measure. God's grace also helped me overcome this weakness. Therefore, if I have successfully completed this book today, it is thanks to God's very special help in my moments of weakness.

As I navigated through life, I have learned to see my sufferings and life challenges as things to get through and adventures to go through. I learned that nothing we go through is wasted. There is always something worth learning from each experience, especially when we give our circumstances to God and let Him shape our perspectives. I learned to cultivate endurance and shift my perspectives. I learned that I can still have peace amidst these problems based on my faith in God, through trusting His process and timing, and, above all, believing His promises. Just because I survived all these experiences does not mean that I did not experience damage. Yes, I did! However, through God's special help and Christ's power, I committed to growth after these traumas. In turn, God gave me a resurrected power that caused me to emerge victorious. I have grown to learn that there is more to us than what we have been through. That is why when I narrate my experiences, I do not narrate them from a defeated or pitiful mindset. Rather, I speak from an overcoming and victorious mindset. Because I overcame them, I believe I will overcome all other challenges that are ahead of me through Christ who strengthens me. I have faith that if I could do these, so could you in Jesus's name. Amen.

Through my life challenges and experiences, God has proven to me that He is the following.

1. El Kanna/The Jealous God, who makes sure that He made everyone I valued more than Him disappoint me (Exodus 20:5).
2. El Shaddai/The All-Sufficient God, who makes me know that when I have Him, I have everything no matter how many enemies teamed up against me (Genesis 17:1).
3. Jehovah Ezrah/My Helper, who sends both angelic and human helpers my way when I feel like giving up (Psalm 27:9).
4. Elohim Shama/The God Who Hears, who heard every cry I offered unto Him (Exodus 2:24).
5. El Roi/The God Who Sees Me, who saw me as something important even when everyone around me saw me as nothing (Genesis 16:13).
6. Elohay Selichot/The God Who Is Ready to Forgive, who forgives my sins even before I could repent or forgive myself (Nehemiah 9:17).
7. El Yeshuati/The God My Salvation, who has delivered me from harm, and sent His only son to die for me cost-free (Isaiah 12:2).
8. Jehovah Gibbor Milchamah/God Mighty in Battle, who gave me victory in all the battles that came my way (Psalm 24:8).
9. El Nathan Neqamah/The God Who Avenges for Me, who raised forth His mighty sword and did not hesitate to strike down anyone who opposed His will in my life (2 Samuel 22:48).
10. Gelah Raz/The Revealer of Mysteries, who gave me revelations about what He was doing or about to do in my life and in the lives of those around me (Daniel 2:28).
11. Elohim Qarob/The God Who Is Near and has always been near me in times of trouble (Deuteronomy 4:7).
12. Shub Nephesh/Renewer of Life, who renewed me when I had given up on myself (Ruth 4:15).

13. Jehovah Jireh/The Lord My Provider, who provided for me in times when I had nothing to show for my efforts (Genesis 22:13–14).
14. Jehovah-Shalom/The Lord Is Peace, who gave me peace amidst the many troubles in my life (Judges 6:24).
15. Jehovah-Makkeh/The God Who Disciplines and did not hesitate to discipline me when I disobeyed Him (Ezekiel 7:9).
16. Jehovah Shammah/God Is There (Present), my ever-present help in time of need (Ezekiel 48:35).
17. El Sela/God My Rock, the God on whom I stood and was never shaken (Psalm 31:3).
18. Jehovah Uzzi/God My Strength, the God who gave me strength in my moments of weakness (Psalm 28:7).
19. El-HaNe'eman/The God Who Is Faithful, who has made sure He kept His covenant to me and to my generations to come (Deuteronomy 7:9).
20. Elohim Ahavah/The God Who Loves Me, who loved me before creation and beyond what I could ever imagine (Jeremiah 31:3).

The list goes on and on.

I am a work in progress, as we all are. Therefore, I believe God will continue to guide us as we strive to express our *authentic* and *true selves* that He created us to express, and as we *soar* through the adversities that life throws at us. I believe that if He could be and do all these for me, He will be and do even more for you both now and beyond in Jesus's name. Amen.

Therefore, I pray that as we strive toward living *authentically* and expressing our *true selves*, God in His infinite mercies will *give us the*

- assurance of Abraham;
- focus of Nehemiah;
- creativity of Gideon;
- innovative skills of Bezalel;
- fearlessness of David;
- meekness of Moses;
- strength of Samson;

- resilience of Ruth;
- good understanding of Abigail;
- obedience of Mary, the mother of Jesus;
- devotion of David;
- conviction of Paul;
- wisdom of Solomon;
- strategy of Elijah;
- empowerment of Esther;
- industrious leadership of Deborah;
- effectiveness of Joseph;
- intelligence and faithfulness of Daniel;
- genius of Jacob;
- diligence of Hannah;
- passion of Peter;
- persistence of Joshua;
- patience of Job;
- obstinate faith in God of Shadrach, Meshach, and Abednego;
- double-fold restorative nature of Job;
- earthly assignment completion of the prophet Samuel; and
- the mind of Christ.

Now unto him that is able to do exceeding abundantly above all that we ask or think, according to the power that worketh in us, unto him be glory in the church by Christ Jesus throughout all ages, world without end. Amen. (Ephesians 3:20–21 KJV).

The Lord bless you and keep you; the Lord makes his face shine upon you and be gracious to you; the Lord lifts up his countenance upon you and gives you peace. So shall they put my name (and your name) upon the people of Israel, and I will bless them. (Numbers 6:24–27 ESV)

Amen.

ACKNOWLEDGMENTS

As I conclude this book, I want to thank my husband Dr. Patrick Bobga for being a listening ear to all my ideas, even when they felt impossible to achieve, and for allowing me to express the full version of myself as we journey through life together. I also want to thank him for staying by me, believing in me, and encouraging me when the cloud was at its darkest.

I want to thank my children Jesse Bobga, Jemimah Bobga, Patrick Jr. Bobga, and Jeremy Bobga for being so patient and understanding in the course of writing this book especially, when Mummy stayed locked up writing instead of taking them to Disneyland or Legoland or other play parks for some fun time together.

I want to thank all the heavenly angels who came to my rescue in my time of need.

I want to thank my guardian angels for constantly coming to fulfill God's promises to me and offering me guidance when I was going astray.

I also want to thank the angels that kept encouraging me when I did not feel like writing or completing this book.

I want to thank all the earthly helpers that God put on my path as I journeyed toward fulfilling His will for my life.

Above all, I want to thank Almighty God for loving me despite my weaknesses and for finding me worthy of completing this assignment even when I did not trust in myself.

BIBLIOGRAPHY

"Alan Cohen Quotes." Quote Fancy. Accessed November 5, 2024. https://quotefancy.com/alan-cohen-quotes.

Appelo, Lisa. "The wilderness is a place of preparation and not permanence." Lisa Appelo. Accessed November 5, 2024. https://lisaappelo.com/3-truths-when-youre-in-the-wilderness/wilderness-a-place-of-preparation-not/.

Batterson, Mark. *Draw the Circle: The 40 Day Prayer Challenge.* Grand Rapids, MI: Zondervan, 2012.

Clauson, Karl. *The 7 Resolutions: Where Self-Help Ends and God's Power Begins.* Chicago, IL: Moody Publishers, 2022.

Foy, Terri Savelle. *Imagine Big: Unlock the Secret to Living Out Your Dreams.* Grand Rapids, MI: Baker Publishing Group, 2013.

———. "Unlocking Your Dreams, Best Vision Board Compilation." YouTube, 47:37, December 2023. https://www.youtube.com/watch?v=CvYQtqZnBw0.

Funke, Felix-Adejumo. Instagram. Accessed November 5, 2024. https://www.instagram.com/reel/C4_Mvf1rfdC/?igsh=MzRlODBiNWFlZA==.

Groeschel, Craig. "Q&A with YouVersion Founder Bobby Gruenewald and Craig Groeschel." YouTube, 21:25. July 31, 2018. https://www.youtube.com/watch?v=1fxPn1JVyks.

Higher Life in Christ. "How to Create A Digital Vision Board in 5 Minutes/ Go After Your Dream Life." YouTube, 6:32, January 2023. https://youtu.be/O7xSHyWu-KQ?si=XW2qElG6VxO-XA2k.

Hudson, Christopher D. *100 Names of God Daily Devotional*. Carol Stream, IL: Rose Publishing, 2021.

Lindbergh, Anne Morrow. "The most exhausting thing you can do is to be inauthentic." The Quotations Page. Accessed November 5, 2024. http://www.quotationspage.com/quote/25698.html.

Moran, Brian P. and Michael Lennington. *The 12-Week Year: Get More Done in 12 Weeks than Others Do in 12 Months*. New York, NY: Wiley, 2013.

"Pamela Short Quotes." Goodreads. Accessed November 5, 2024. https://www.goodreads.com/author/quotes/14997571.Pamela_Short.

Schwarzenegger, Arnold. "Create a vision of who you want to be, and then live into that picture as if it were already true." AZ Quotes. Accessed November 5, 2024. https://www.azquotes.com/quote/835670#google_vignette.

Shaurya, Vikrant. *How to Write a Bestseller: Become a Bestselling Author, Attract High-Value Clients, and Skyrocket Your Authority*, n.p. 2020.

"Steve Maraboli Quotes." Goodreads. Accessed November 5, 2024. https://www.goodreads.com/author/quotes/4491185.Steve_Maraboli.

TerKeurst, Lysa. *Forgiving What You Can't Forget: Discover How to Move On, Make Peace with Painful Memories, and Create a Life That's Beautiful Again*. Nashville, TN: Thomas Nelson, 2020.

Trimm, Cindy. *Hello, Tomorrow!: The Transformational Power of Vision*. Lake Mary, FL: Charisma, 2018.

Trimm Cindy. "Next-Level Thinking [The Power of Intention] Dr. Cindy Trimm" YouTube, 1:03:19. July 14, 2022. https://youtu.be/xiuTM0r6YiU?si=8SPUa5NXPKX0LsMg.

Trimm, Cindy. *Unstoppable: Compete with Your Best Self and Win*. Stockbridge, GA: Cindy Trimm, 2021.